THE

INNER
BONDING

. . . .

GUIDED
JOURNAL

. . . .

THE

INNER
BONDING

. . . .

GUIDED
JOURNAL

. . . .

**YOUR COMPLETE TOOL FOR AN
INSPIRED, PEACEFUL & JOYOUS LIFE**

Margaret Paul, PhD,
& Erika Chopich, PhD,
with Ivana Polonijo, PhD

&
MEDIA

INNER BONDING®
The Power to Heal Yourself

Courageous Being

MEDIA

Published 2024 by Gildan Media LLC
aka G&D Media
www.GandDmedia.com

Design by Kristin Anderson.
Thanks to Scott Friedman for eagle-eye edits.

Library of Congress Cataloging-in-Publication Data is available upon request

ISBN: 978-1-7225-0720-6

10 9 8 7 6 5 4 3 2 1

TOOLS
& PROMPTS

DAILY
INNER BONDING®
PRACTICE

NAME

DATE

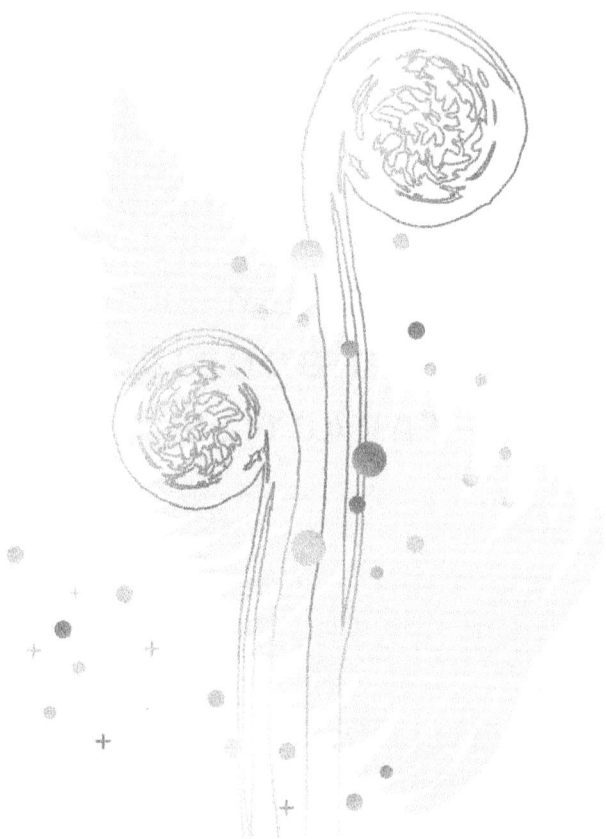

Let this journal be your guide to a deeper and more meaningful Inner Bonding Practice

. . . .

WITH CONSISTENT PRACTICE,
INNER BONDING CAN HELP YOU
DISCOVER WHO YOU REALLY ARE,
HEAL YOUR FALSE BELIEFS,
CONNECT WITH A HIGHER SOURCE
OF LOVE AND TRUTH ON DEMAND,
AND DEVELOP A POWERFUL
LOVING SELF WHO CAN
TAKE GREAT CARE OF YOU
AND YOUR ENVIRONMENT
IN ANY SITUATION.

. . . .

. . . .

DEAR
JOURNALER,

. . . .

When you open this journal, you stand at the threshold
of the enduring power that Inner Bonding holds.

With practice, it will help the essence of your being
shine with self-love and self-awareness.

As you practice daily, remember that practice is the
heartbeat of transformation and know that you are not alone.
You are held within the embrace of a community that
spans generations, individuals who have discovered the
strength that comes from unearthing their authentic selves.

Let this journal be your companion, your confidant, and your
mirror—reflecting back the beauty that lies within you.

We are sending you our love and our blessings,

. . . .

MARGARET & ERIKA

Table of Contents

Why waste any energy
on changing what you
cannot change—
others and outcomes.

Better to spend your
energy changing what
you can change, which
is you—your intent.

MARGARET & ERIKA

Inner
Bonding
Basics

Inner Bonding
Introduction

. . . .

INNER BONDING IS A STEP-BY-STEP
PROCESS THAT ENABLES YOU TO
SELF-HEAL ROOT CAUSES OF ISSUES
STANDING IN THE WAY OF YOUR
GROWTH AND SATISFACTION.

IT HAS BEEN DEVELOPED AND
OPTIMIZED OVER 40 YEARS BY
DR. MARGARET PAUL AND
DR. ERIKA CHOPICH.

WHEN YOU PRACTICE IT DAILY,
INNER BONDING HELPS YOU SHIFT
OUT OF VICTIM CONSCIOUSNESS,
TAKE RESPONSIBILITY FOR YOUR FEELINGS
AND BECOME A POWERFUL, LOVING BEING
WHO KNOWS HOW TO LOVE YOURSELF,
STOP SELF-SABOTAGING BEHAVIORS,
CREATE LOVING RELATIONSHIPS,
AND ADDRESS ANY ISSUES STEMMING
FROM SELF-ABANDONMENT.

THE PROCESS IS COMPREHENSIVE.
IT'S PRACTICAL.
AND IT ALWAYS WORKS—
WHEN YOU DO IT.

It All Starts
With a Choice

Intent

Our intent is what governs how we think, feel and behave. It is a powerful and creative force—the essence of free will. Your intent is your deepest desire, your primary motive or goal, your highest priority in any given moment.

Inner Bonding process teaches that there are only **two primary intents:**

- To **learn about loving yourself and others**, even in the face of fear and pain.
- To **protect yourself from fear and pain** with addictive, controlling behavior and thereby avoid responsibility for your feelings and actions.

When your intent is to LEARN TO LOVE, you are willing to face fears and feel painful feelings in order to compassionately nurture them, or understand how you may be creating them, and discover what you need to do differently. The deeper purpose here is to become a more loving human being, starting with yourself. When you open to learning about your own fears and beliefs and about what brings you joy, you move toward love. Your deepest desire is to find your safety, peace, lovability and worth through an *internal* connection with the unconditional love that is available on the spiritual level.

When your intent is to PROTECT YOURSELF from fear and pain through some form of control, and avoid responsibility for your feelings, your deepest desire is to find your safety, peace, lovability and worth through *externals*, such as attention, approval, sex, substances, material things, and activities.

When you believe that others are responsible for how you feel, you try to control them in order to feel safe and worthy. In every moment, each one of us chooses our intent—either to attempt to feel externally safe by controlling others and our own feelings, or to create inner safety by learning about loving ourselves and others. **While the choices that others make may influence you, no one but you has control over your intent.** Not even spirit, the source, or higher power can control your intent, since that would negate your free will. In each moment, you choose what is most important to you, and in each moment you have an opportunity to change your mind.

False Beliefs

Growing up, we all absorbed false beliefs that cause us to abandon ourselves. Often they are background noise—subconscious lies we tell ourselves that create unnecessary suffering, anxiety, depression, shame or other painful wounded feelings. We then slip into the intent to protect against the fear and pain caused by false beliefs by sinking into various forms of self-abandonment (see page 20 to learn how to distinguish between wounded and core feelings).

GOLDEN NUGGET

If you have been living from the intent to control for most of your life, it will take time to create a new default of living from the intent to learn. Don't get discouraged!

TAKING LOVING CARE OF YOURSELF IS A LIFELONG PROCESS!

The Big Four

INNER BONDING PARTS OF CONSCIOUSNESS

. . . .

The Inner Bonding process works with different parts of our consciousness. It's important to understand their differences.

Inner Child

Inner Child represents the *feeling* aspect of us located in the body who spontaneously expresses love, curiosity, passion, creativity and feelings of joy and sorrow. When our Inner Child is free to express themself, we are creative, trusting in ourselves, authentic, honest, living in peace, joy and gratitude, feeling generous, free, whole and fulfilled. We can also refer to this part as true or authentic self, our essence, our soul in the body.

PRIMARY CONCERN:
How can I best **express who I am and my unique innate gifts**?
How can I walk the path of freedom to be fully myself?

Wounded Self

Wounded Self is a programmed, conditioned *thought* process located in the lower left brain. Its intention is to control external circumstances and other people. This aspect operates from fear and false beliefs and is always on the lookout to avoid pain. It is incapable of connecting to a source of truth and love and it protects against pain with addictive behaviors. It resists surrendering to higher Guidance— then feels alone so has to control everything to try to feel safe.

PRIMARY CONCERN:
How can I **get love** and **avoid pain** so that I **feel safe**?

Loving Adult

Loving Adult is a state we embody when we operate from our heart, connected with love, wisdom, truth, courage, strength of spirit. You can think of this aspect as a vehicle through which the universal source of compassion operates in this physical body to put love into action. Loving Adult is willing to take responsibility for feelings of pain, joy and safety, opens to learning with the Inner Child, Wounded Self, Guidance and others, explores and heals false beliefs through receiving truth from Guidance and taking loving action.

PRIMARY CONCERN:
How can I best **give love**—to myself and to others?

Guidance

The energy of unconditional love, truth, wisdom, peace and joy available to all of us in the spiritual realm when we learn/remember how to access it. Information coming through your mind from your **personal experience of spirit**, source, higher self, the universe, the divine, universal energy, presence, God, Goddess, guardian angel, saint, mentor, light or even older wiser part of yourself, say three hundred years from now!

GOLDEN NUGGET

Remember that your Wounded Self is a false sense of self. It's important not to feed it, not to give it power. Watch out for indulging it! If you feel it's getting louder and overwhelming you with false beliefs, focus more on connecting with Guidance.

Six Steps of Inner Bonding

STEP 1

Get present with your feelings. Tend to your physical sensations and feelings as if you were looking after a child. If a child is upset, you don't walk away, you sit down with them and listen. We practice doing this with ourselves, moving toward our feelings with compassion, with a desire to take responsibility for what's going on inside us.

STEP 2

Choose the intention to learn about loving yourself. This is where we invite in the presence of Guidance—of higher love, wisdom, courage and comfort of spirit. This is a simple invitation but immensely powerful—opening to learning with spirit is what creates our Loving Adult self.

STEP 3

Have compassionate dialogue with your Inner Child and your Wounded Self. In this step we explore the beliefs that are fueling our behaviors and look at where they came from. We also connect with our gifts and what brings joy to our inner child.

STEP 4

Dialogue with your higher self / Guidance. We ask for the truth about any false beliefs we've discovered, and we ask for what would be loving to us—what is in our highest good.

STEP 5

Take action. Whatever guidance you received, act on it. Whether it's as simple as going to bed earlier tonight or as challenging as speaking up for yourself in a relationship, it's key to follow through.

STEP 6

Evaluate the effectiveness of your action. Check in with yourself to see how you're feeling. Are you feeling some relief, less shame, less emptiness? If not, go through the process again.

Review **Bridges to Learning** overview on pages 24–25 to help you get into your body and open to conducting the process and taking responsibility for your feelings.

If anger is getting in the way of your willingness to open to learning with curiosity, try the **Three-Part Anger Process** outlined on pages 26–27.

Check out the **Full Process** on pages 36–41 to get a clear sense of key prompts and review a process example.

Is your **frequency perhaps too low?** Review pages 22–23 and learn about three key areas we all need to pay attention to as we work on improving our overall health and wellness.

In the **Notes** section starting on page 117, you can keep lists of different discoveries you make as you practice: characteristics of your Essence and Guidance, situations you want to work on, your loving actions.

Explore the list of many **Resources** on page 139 that you can turn to as you look to deepen or expand your Inner Bonding Practice.

Painful Feelings— Core or Wounded?

. . . .

When you practice Inner Bonding daily, you can heal deep internal wounds and address the root cause of issues such as anxiety, stress, depression, low self-worth, addictions, and/or relationship problems. When you create a profound connection with your true self, spirit, and others, you'll unleash creativity, imagination, passion, purpose, love and joy! This all sounds great, but most of us are so used to abandoning ourselves in some way that it will take some time and dedicated practice and effort to stop the default behaviors.

Here are four major ways we tend to abandon ourselves:

1. We stay up in our head. We've learned to stay in our head as a way of protecting against pain. That's why Step 1 is about getting into your body.

2. We judge ourselves. We run programmed thoughts in our head like "You are not good enough." This is one of the major, common judgments, but there are many others we make against ourselves.

3. We turn to addictions to numb out our feelings. Remember that we're not just talking about classic addictions like alcohol and nicotine here. Anything can become an addiction, depending on our intent.

4. We make others responsible for whether or not we are okay. Wounded thought patterns in this case sound like "If I am a good person, other people will like me, and then I'll be okay."

Understanding the contrast between wounded feelings and core painful feelings is crucial to understanding why we ever engage in self-abandonment.

Core painful feelings—loneliness, heartache, grief, sorrow, helplessness over others, and fear of real and present danger—reflect current external reality. They are telling us something external is occurring that is causing these feelings—there is no one to connect with, or the person you are with is shut down; someone is being unloving to you, to themselves, or to someone else; something tragic has happened; something dangerous is about to happen.

Wounded feelings, by contrast, are based on the false beliefs we absorbed from past reality. They are often linked to childhood traumatic experiences. When someone today behaves towards us unlovingly, wounded feelings like shame or guilt may arise, driven by false beliefs such as "I don't matter." They are not based on current reality but on internalized false beliefs.

Where things get tricky is when core painful feelings emerge from real, current situations, but instead of fully feeling them we instead—by default, unconsciously—start masking them with wounded feelings fueled by false beliefs.

For example, your past reality might have been that you were in some way harmed by your caregivers. Because you were too small to feel your core pain over these experiences at the time, you likely established some false beliefs, such as that the abuse was your fault because you are not good enough. Today, if someone is being unloving to you, instead of feeling a core painful feeling like loneliness or helplessness over their behavior, you might be telling yourself an internalized lie that they are being unloving because you are not lovable enough—that it's your fault that they are being mean. Underneath your wounded feelings may be core feelings, and you might be avoiding them with one or more types of self-abandonment.

GOLDEN NUGGET

By practicing Inner Bonding, managing core painful feelings becomes easier, reducing the frequency and intensity of wounded feelings.

How High is Your Frequency?

Frequency: Key to Connecting With Guidance

Nikola Tesla said: "If you want to find the secrets of the universe, think in terms of energy, frequency and vibration." All matter is made up of energy. Energy vibrates, and the higher the vibration of the energy, the higher the frequency. All atoms, protons, and neutrons vibrate at a particular frequency. Everything in the universe has a vibrational frequency, including you. Your connection with Guidance occurs when your vibrancy and frequency is raised enough to make you energetically available to the higher vibration of Guidance.

If you walk into a room full of angry, blaming people, you might feel a heavy, dark energy in the room and start feeling anxious or depressed. That's a low frequency. If you walk into a room of open and caring people, you will likely feel relaxed due to the light, vibrant energy in the room. That's a high frequency. Frequency is a delicate thing. Many situations, both physical and emotional, affect your frequency. Here are some examples of what can lower your frequency:

- Intent to Control, Negative Thinking/Talking, Resistance
- Exhaustion
- Illness
- Poor Nutrition
- Alcohol & Drugs
- Lack of Exercise
- Negative Environment

Love, compassion, joy and inner peace are the highest frequency feelings. Being kind and compassionate with yourself and others creates inner peace, which raises your frequency. Genuine, heart-felt gratitude and laughter are both ways you will always raise your frequency!

Three Pillars of Health and Wellness

THREE KEY PILLARS PROMOTING OVERALL WELL-BEING, HEALTHY LIFESTYLE AND HIGH FREQUENCY

1. Nutrition Plus! = anything you ingest (so, it will need to be digested)

This pillar is primarily about nutrition, food and healthy eating, but can be anything else we consume or have to process with our physical/emotional/mental body, like substances, environmental phenomena (polluted air), noise . . . And let's not forget technology, screen time, social media consumption!

2. Balanced Movement = sleep and exercise

This pillar is about harmonious integration of both active motion and relaxation. Striking a balance between movement and rest, sleep and exercise is crucial for maintaining physical, mental, and emotional health.

3. Inner Bonding

This pillar involves practicing the 6-step process on a regular basis to gain a deeper understanding of our thoughts, emotions, and behaviors, uncover limiting beliefs and patterns, foster greater self-awareness and emotional intelligence, and learn loving actions to help us effectively manage stress, conflicts, and challenges.

. . . . GOLDEN NUGGET . . . .

When you attempt Inner Bonding from a low frequency, it will be much harder to connect with your Guidance. Do something from the first two pillars of health that raises your frequency, then come back and do the process.

If You Are Closed, Here's How to Get Open

Bridges to Learning

When you are stuck in the anger, blame, depression or numbness of your Wounded Self, you need to find a bridge that will take you into a state of openness to learning.

Bridges are things you can do to open your heart. Of the many bridges you can use, prayer, especially a prayer of gratitude, is probably the most powerful bridge. Prayer can take many forms, such as dialogue, meditation, recitation or song. The choice is up to you. Some people have found that repeating a simple prayer of gratitude throughout the day helps them stay open to learning.

Generosity is another bridge to opening the heart. Many of us focus on how we can get what we want or avoid getting hurt. But one of the quickest ways of moving out of a closed heart and into openness is to ask your Guidance: "What can I give to myself and others?" The moment you sincerely ask this question—with no attachment to its outcome—your heart will open and love will rush in, just as air rushes into your lungs the moment you take a breath.

This happens because the very nature of Guidance is abundant, unconditionally loving and always here for you when you ask for help. When you walk in thinking, "What can I give? I can give people my smile, my interest, my acceptance and my sense of humor," you will feel great. The moment you decide to give, your heart opens.

If the notion of prayer doesn't work for you, for whatever reason, there are many other bridges to try that can open your heart to learning about love. These include:

- Listening to music

- Taking a walk

- Being in nature

- Talking with a friend

- Reading spiritual literature

- Journaling

- Drawing or doing other artwork like sculpture or collage

- Dancing

- Attending Twelve Step or other support group meetings

- Playing with a child or a pet

- Being held by a loving person

- Letting yourself cry

- Releasing your anger alone by doing an Inner Bonding Anger Process

GOLDEN NUGGET

When you act from a state of gratitude, you move out of acting from a place of lack and desperation for control. By saying a simple "thank you" for something or someone in your life, you create a state of peacefulness that invites Guidance in.

The Three-Part Anger Process

We use the Inner Bonding Anger Process to move out of being angry at others and feeling like a victim, and into personal responsibility. The Anger Process is part of Step Two of Inner Bonding. It is a powerful way to release anger that may be in the way of being open to learning. It is a three-part process.

Releasing your anger will work only when your intent behind doing the Anger Process is to learn about what you do that causes your angry feelings. If you just want to use your anger to blame, control, and justify your position, you will stay stuck in your anger, stuck with a closed heart.

At its root, anger at another person is generally a projection of your Inner Child's anger at you for not taking loving care of yourself. Recognizing your anger at others as a projection can move you into an intent to learn.

People who consistently practice Inner Bonding find themselves feeling less angry. As they develop their Loving Adult, they find that they no longer take others' behavior personally, even when someone is angry or disapproving. As they learn to take responsibility for their own feelings, they stop blaming others for their painful feelings. As they learn to define their own worth through their connection with spirit, they are no longer so reactive to others' disapproval.

...... GOLDEN NUGGET ....

Anger is different than feeling outrage at a situation. Anger covers up the fear of feeling painful feelings, while outrage calls you to act when you witness a horrible situation, such as a child being abused, or face someone who is physically threatening you. In these times, outrage invokes the power of Guidance and inspires strong loving action.

This three-part anger process moves you out of victim mode into openheartedness. It is not closed anger; this is anger that is open to learning and results in awareness of what you are doing that your Inner Child is angry about at you. Find a safe and quiet place to do this.

1. **Imagine that the person you are angry at is sitting in front of you.** Let your Inner Child yell at him or her, saying in detail everything you wish you could say. Unleash your anger, pain and resentment until you have nothing more to say. You can scream and cry, pound a pillow, roll up a towel and beat the bed. (The reason you don't tell the person directly is because this kind of cathartic, no-holds-barred "anger dump" would be abusive to them.)

2. **Now ask yourself who this person reminds you of in your past.** Your mother or father, a grandparent, a sibling? (It may be the same person. That is, you may be mad at your father now, and he is acting just like he did when you were little.) Now let your Inner Child yell at the person from the past as thoroughly and energetically as in part one.

3. **Finally, come back into the present and let your Inner Child do the same thing with you, expressing your Inner Child's anger, pain and resentment toward you for your part in the situation or for treating yourself the way the people in parts one and two treated you.** This brings the problem home to personal responsibility, opening the door to exploring your own behavior.

Remember that the Anger Process is part of Step 2 of Inner Bonding, so once you successfully use it to get yourself open to learning, continue going through the rest of the steps, starting with Step 3.

Process for Being With Your Core Painful Feelings

It is important to learn to lovingly manage your existential pain. Releasing the feelings stuck in your body promotes good health, heals addictions, reduces wounded feelings, and invites a deeper sense of your purpose and passion.

Put your hands on your heart

1: Compassionately embrace your feelings of loneliness, grief, heartache, heartbreak, helplessness over others, sadness, sorrow, or fear of real and present danger. Be very gentle, tender, caring and understanding with yourself . . . these painful feelings require your willingness to fully feel them.

2: When you are ready to release the feelings, give them to Guidance and invite in peace and acceptance. It helps to say it out loud: *"I release this situation and give it over to you, Guidance, and receive peace and acceptance from you in return."*

3: Open to learning what these feelings are telling you about what is happening with someone or with an event or situation—they are good information!

4: Open to learning with your Guidance about the loving action you can take in this situation.

5: Take the loving action. This is key.

6: Evaluate how you are feeling as a result of taking the loving action.

What if the Process Didn't Work

If you've done the process more than once exploring the same situation, but you feel like it didn't work, consider the possibility that your frequency is too low.

See page 22 and explore ideas for raising your vibration: take a walk, take a shower, make sure you are appropriately full of good, nutritious food. If you are feeling lonely, talk to someone, and focus on connecting with Guidance.

If you are still not getting anywhere despite working on raising your frequency, it's probably time to ask a facilitator for help. Remember that there are low-cost and even free facilitation support options available on the Inner Bonding website (www.innerbonding.com).

Process for When You're Feeling Great!

We can do the Inner Bonding process at any time, not just in times of distress. In those instances when you are feeling relaxed, at ease, confident, poised, **follow the traditional Steps 1 and 2**.

When you get to **Step 3, focus on asking your Inner Child what SPECIFICALLY you are no longer doing, or have started doing, that's contributing to the wonderful feelings.** Chances are, your Inner Child has started trusting you, is enjoying your loving-adult maturity, the love you're sharing with other people, blossoming creativity, increase in energy. Ask your Inner Child what else he/she would enjoy doing? Anything they want to experience, try, explore, create?

You can also conduct **Step 4, opening to Guidance to learn additional loving actions you can take** to foster the beautiful bond you're cultivating with your Inner Child and Spirit. Remember to **follow through and take the action in Step 5, then evaluate in Step 6.**

Resistance to Practicing: Explore It to Dissolve It

· · · · · · · · · · · ·

We often hear people say: "I understand Inner Bonding intellectually, but I don't remember to do it." Inner Bonding is akin to a workout routine—it's not enough to understand it intellectually; you must actually do the process in order to "develop some muscle" and receive benefits.

If you are resistant to practicing, there are good reasons for it. Actually, exploring your resistance is part of the practice.

Here are some of the typical reasons why you might be avoiding doing Inner Bonding:

- **If I open to my feelings, they might overwhelm me.**
  If this is your fear, consider trauma therapies (for example, Emotional Freedom Technique or Somatic Experiencing) to lessen feeling intensity and learn emotional regulation. Cultivating a spiritual connection is also important—it is your connection to your source of love and comfort that enables you to lovingly manage your painful feelings.

- **I forget to do it.**
  This is so common! Most of us forget to do the actual steps in real time when we're first getting started with our practice. We are so used to avoiding our feelings that we find ourselves automatically turning to our traditional protections/addictions rather than turning to Inner Bonding. Find physical ways to remind yourself to stay in Step One: set an alarm on your cell phone, wear a rubber band on your wrist, use sticky notes to remind yourself to tune into your body.

- **I'm afraid I can't do it "right."**

  Your wounded self might define your worth in terms of whether you do things "right" or "wrong," rather than in terms of the effort you make. Explore your fear of not doing something "right." What happened to you as a child when you made mistakes? Do you currently judge yourself for mistakes and failures, or are you able to learn from them?

- **I don't have the time and it's too much work.**

  It takes less time and energy to love yourself than it does to abandon yourself. Think about all the time and energy you might be taking up by judging yourself, ruminating and figuring things out in your head, turning to your various addictions, and all the controlling things you do to try to get others' approval.

- **I don't want to be controlled by my Guidance.**

  Since the Wounded Self is the part of us that wants control, you might feel threatened by opening to learning with your Guidance. With practice, Wounded Self will start to feel relief at not having to try to control everything. Instead, Guidance alleviates the burden of trying to control everything. Knowing you're guided toward your highest good fosters a great sense of relief!

······· GOLDEN NUGGET ···

Practicing Inner Bonding is not about doing it "right." It's about gradually healing your false beliefs that limit you, and learning to take loving care of yourself. There is no objective right or wrong way to do this. You know you are doing it right for you when you feel lighter, happier and more peaceful.

Your experience of others and outcomes will change when you become who you came here to become— a loving, giving, peaceful, joyful, and creative human being.

MARGARET & ERIKA

Inner Bonding Full Process

Full Process Introduction

INSIDE THIS SECTION, YOU WILL FIND
DETAILED PROMPTS TO GO THROUGH
THE INNER BONDING PROCESS.

WITH PRACTICE, YOU CAN LEARN
TO TURN TO THE SIX STEPS ANY TIME YOU FEEL
ANYTHING OTHER THAN PEACE INSIDE.

WHEN WE FEEL ANYTHING LESS THAN
INNER PEACE, OUR INNER CHILD IS GIVING US
INFORMATION, AND WE NEED TO LEARN
TO ATTEND TO IT AS A LOVING ADULT.

IT TAKES PRACTICE TO BECOME PRESENT.
YOU ARE ESSENTIALLY REWIRING
YOUR BRAIN'S NEUROLOGICAL PATHWAYS
THAT RUN ON SELF-ABANDONING DEFAULTS
SO YOU CAN START LIVING YOUR LIFE
WITH JOY, EASE AND FULFILLMENT.

TO DOWNLOAD BLANK TEMPLATES OF THE
PRACTICE SPREADS, SCAN THIS QR CODE

Full Process

—SIX STEPS OF INNER BONDING—

. . . .

CONSIDER READING THESE DETAILED PROMPTS
OUT LOUD AND RECORDING IT, SO YOU CAN LISTEN TO
THEM WHEN YOU PRACTICE AND SELF-FACILITATE

STEP 1   Be Willing to Take Responsibility for All of Your Feelings

Take some deep breaths. Use your breath to go inside and scan your body. Notice what's happening inside, right now. **Is there anything you are picking up on with your bodily sensations other than peace and fullness?** Remember that this is how your Inner Child communicates with you, letting you know that something needs attending to. Breathe into the sensation and get present with it. Make a decision you want responsibility for this feeling, this sensation. Do so even if you notice a good feeling—there is much you can learn about what you're doing to cause the pleasant sensation. Welcome and embrace all feelings with compassion.

WRITE DOWN WHAT YOU NOTICED:

> *Example: Tight throat, pressure in my chest; the throat sensation feels "stronger."*

CAN YOU MAKE A DECISION THAT YOU WANT RESPONSIBILITY
FOR YOUR FEELINGS?

> *Example: I am willing to take 100% responsibility for my feelings, for the tight throat, pressure in my chest.*

If you are willing, then go to Step 2.

If you are unwilling, explore the good reasons—your fears and beliefs—preventing you from being willing. Consider using some Bridges to Learning (see pages 24–25).

---

2 Move Into the Intent to Learn

Breathe into your heart, getting present in your heart, making a choice of intention, **consciously choosing to be open to learning.** Move into compassionate curiosity about how you're treating yourself, what you're telling yourself; what you are doing or not doing to be causing the feelings you noticed in Step 1. You are not doing any exploring in this step—you are simply **making a decision to open to learning about your false beliefs or core feelings, about what's true, and about what would be loving to you.**

NOW VISUALIZE YOUR HIGHER GUIDANCE—HOWEVER YOU IMAGINE THAT—AND JUST SAY OUT LOUD OR WRITE DOWN: "I INVITE YOUR LOVE, YOUR COMPASSION, YOUR STRENGTH, YOUR WISDOM, YOUR COURAGE, YOUR TRUTH INTO MY HEART."

> *Example: I invite the love, compassion, strength, wisdom of my older wiser self into my heart.*

You are a Loving Adult when you are open to learning, connected to Guidance, and filled with compassion and curiosity about the very good reasons you are feeling and behaving the way you are. If that's not happening, you are not in a Loving Adult state, you are in Wounded Self.

STEP
3

Dialogue With Inner Child
& Wounded Self

Breathe back into your feelings. First, tune into your Inner Child. If you are aware of something other than peace and fullness, ask your Inner Child **what *you* are doing to be causing the feelings and sensations you identified in Step 1—*not* what's happening externally.** You are looking to learn what you are telling yourself from your Wounded Self, how you're treating yourself from your Wounded Self. Go in and listen. Let your Inner Child tell you what you might be doing that's self-abandoning. Maybe you are applying some kind of internal pressure on yourself, maybe you are being judgmental, or staying in your head, or numbing out with addictions, or perhaps you are emotionally giving your Inner Child away to somebody else instead of taking care of him or her within. So listen.

WHAT IS YOUR INNER CHILD TELLING YOU?
LET THEM WRITE THE ANSWER HERE, IN FIRST PERSON.

Example: You are telling me that we can't speak up about this situation. The project at work is too much for us; you are pushing me to complete it by myself and won't ask anyone for help. You are scaring me, saying to me on the inside that if we ask for help, we'll get in trouble. That doesn't feel good! You are hurting me when you say unloving things like, we have to work harder, or when you don't let us go to sleep because you want us to finish this project before the boss asks about it. You are stressing me out!

If your Inner Child shares information about the ways in which you are abandoning yourself, go a little deeper, into the Wounded Self: it's your wounded ego that's doing the self-abandoning. Again, go in and listen. Let your Wounded Self tell you why they are "kicking in." There must be a very good reason that you are putting pressure on yourself, or staying in your head, numbing out with addictions . . . Listen to that programmed Wounded Self—it has many false beliefs and this is how you become aware of them, so you can dissolve and heal them. You can let the Wounded Self write the answer here, in first person. Pay attention to how old this voice is—it's likely pretty young.

WHAT IS YOUR WOUNDED SELF TELLING YOU?

> *Example: We have to work hard to make sure we keep this job! We need it! What would happen if we lost the income? It would be just like when dad lost his job and we didn't have any money and everything at home was gloomy and sad and scary and uncomfortable . . . I never want to feel anything like that again. If we ask for help, the boss will think we don't know how to do our job, and they'll fire us.*

If your process uncovers that you are dealing with existential feelings of life— grief, heartache, loneliness, helplessness over somebody else—put your hands on your heart, bring in compassion and sit with the feelings until they are ready to move through for this time. You may need to repeat this process.

LET YOUR INNER CHILD KNOW SHE/HE IS NOT ALONE:

> *Example: I hear you, Little One. I know that the boss can sometimes be harsh in the way they talk about deadlines. It hurts our heart when they are uncaring. We don't have any control over that, but I am here for you. You are not alone.*

Dialogue With Guidance

Once you've uncovered what's going on, **visualize yourself in a beautiful place in nature with your higher self,** however you visualize that, and ask your Guidance from a place of deep curiosity: what is the truth about any false belief that you connected with when dialoguing with your Wounded Self? Ask your Guidance to tell you the truth about all the information you became aware of in Step 3. Listen. If it feels like you are making it up, that's okay. See if you can suspend the disbelief and allow for the possibility that the information coming through can be very useful. Guidance speaks in many ways—words, pictures, feelings.

WHAT DOES GUIDANCE SAY IS THE TRUTH ABOUT THIS SITUATION?

Example: This situation is nothing like the past. Being honest with your boss about your bandwidth and setting realistic expectations shows maturity as a worker and is valuable to the company. Also—if you did lose your job for some reason, you can handle it. This isn't likely, but if it came to pass, we would look for another job and be able to deal with it.

Next ask your Guidance, what would be loving to your Inner Child right in this moment. What does your Inner Child need from you? Again listen.

WHAT DOES GUIDANCE SAY WOULD BE LOVING TO YOUR INNER CHILD RIGHT NOW?

Example: Email your boss tomorrow and ask for a meeting to discuss the project timeline and involving others to help.

5 Take Loving Action

If it's something you can do right now—do it! If it isn't, then imagine doing it.

CAN YOU TAKE THE LOVING ACTION? IF NOT, USE THIS SPACE TO IMAGINE DOING IT, OR PLAN WHEN YOU WILL DO IT.

> *Example: I can write a draft email tonight and prepare it so I can simply press the "Send" button in the morning. I'll keep my comments concise, giving the boss a quick overview of the project's current status and offering a few options for meeting date and time.*

STEP

6 Evaluate the Action

Now tune into how you feel as a result of taking the loving action.

HAVE YOU TAKEN THE LOVING ACTION?
HOW DO YOU FEEL NOW?

> *Example: I haven't sent the email yet, but I already feel better. There is still some tightness in my throat—my Inner Child doesn't fully trust yet that I'll take the action. But it's not as bad as when I started the process! And the pressure in my chest is gone!*

TO DOWNLOAD BLANK TEMPLATES OF THE PRACTICE SPREADS, SCAN THIS QR CODE

Dialogue Questions

PROMPTS TO HELP YOU WITH INNER DIALOGUING

When doing an Inner Bonding process, it's important not to skip any steps. The more you practice them, the more natural it will be to do them in order. As you learn and practice, take the time to do each step fully before moving on to the next step. This will help you get better at discerning the difference between the voice of your Inner Child, your Wounded Self, and your Guidance.

Here are some additional prompts to help you with Step 1 and Step 2, followed by questions you can use in the dialogue processes as part of Step 3 and Step 4.

Before You Start Dialoguing:
Start with Step 1: Breathe into your body and scan your body for physical sensations. In this way, you are getting present with your feelings in the body. Make a conscious decision that you want responsibility for the sensations and feelings you are experiencing.

Move into Step 2: Start by placing a hand on your heart, and again use the breath—breathe into your heart. As you do so, consciously choose the intent to learn about loving yourself. Invite the presence of your Guidance (the presence of love, compassion, strength, courage, wisdom . . .) into your heart.

Now that you have invited Guidance to be with you as you explore, you can be a Loving Adult as you dialogue with your Inner Child and Wounded Self.

Prompts for Dialoguing with Your Inner Child

The Loving Adult asks the Inner Child in Step 3:

- What are you feeling right now?

- What am I telling you that is causing these feelings?

- How am I treating you that is causing these feelings?

- What am I doing or not doing that is causing you to feel this way?

- How am I abandoning you?

- How am I rejecting you?

- Am I judging you?

- Am I scaring you with lies or false beliefs?

- Am I turning to addictions to numb out your feelings?

- Am I giving you away to others, making others responsible for you?

- Are you angry with me? It's okay to be angry with me. I'd like to hear your anger.

- I'd like to understand why you feel scared of _____.

- I'd like to understand why you don't like _____.

- I'd like to understand how you feel about _____.

- Is something happening now that reminds you of something that happened when we were little?

- Do you need to be held while you're going through this pain?

- It's okay to cry. I am here for you.

Prompts for Dialoguing with Your Wounded Self

The Loving Adult asks the Wounded Self in Step 3:

- What are you trying to control or avoid by ignoring our feelings?

- What are you trying to control or avoid by judging, staying in your mind, turning to addictions, and/or making others responsible for our feelings?

- What is your belief about your ability to handle pain (or about your lovability, your ability to control others, your feeling responsible for others, others' responsibility for you, your right to make yourself happy, your ability to make yourself happy . . .)?

- Where did you get this belief?

- What childhood experiences created this belief?

- What do you gain by acting as if this belief were true?

- What are you afraid of in letting go of this belief?

- What are you afraid would happen if you stopped acting as if this belief were true?

Prompts for Dialoguing with Guidance

The Loving Adult asks Guidance in Step 4:

- What is the truth about the beliefs I have uncovered?

- What is the loving action toward my Inner Child?

- What do I need to think or do differently to take care of my Inner Child?

- What is the real issue here?

- What do I need to look at about myself?

- What is my responsibility in this situation?

Affirmations to Offer to Your Inner Child

At times during the dialogue in Step 3 you as the Loving Adult may need to affirm how you feel about your Inner Child. You can use these statements to validate your Inner Child—your essence.

- I'm here for you right now, and I'm learning to be present for you.

- I love you, and your happiness is the most important thing in the world to me.

- You are so smart. Thank you for all this wonderful wisdom.

- Your creativity amazes me.

- It's truly okay for you to feel this anger, even if it's at me. I won't stop loving you no matter how angry you feel.

- You can keep crying as long as you need to. You're not alone. I'm here for you.

- It's okay to make mistakes. You are loveable even if you make mistakes.

- You don't have to do it "right." I will continue to love you no matter what you say or do, even if you say or do nothing at all.

GOLDEN NUGGET

Remember that none of the dialoguing questions we suggest in this section are set in stone. Feel free to create your own. The process is about you tuning into your unique essence, and addressing it with the specific questions that work best for you!

Questions to Use to Get to Know Your Inner Child Really Well!

The dialogue process can help you become aware of what your Inner Child loves in the world and wants or prefers in everyday situations. Discover more about your Inner Child's worldview by asking the following questions.

- What would you like to eat today?
  (What would you like for breakfast / lunch / dinner / snack?)

- What are your favorite foods?

- What kind of exercise do you like?

- What do you feel like wearing today?

- What are your favorite colors?

- What kind of books do you like to read?

- What kind of music do you like?

- What kind of movies do you like?

- What would you like to do this evening / this weekend / for this upcoming vacation?

- What kind of creative things do you like to do? Art? Crafts? Musing? Writing?

- What are your favorite activities to do?

- What are some things you've always wanted to do but have never done?

- Who do you like to spend time with?

Questions to Begin Discovering Your Passionate Purpose

At a time when you know you are in your Loving Adult state and you are feeling peaceful and connected with your Inner Child and Your Guidance, ask your Inner Child:

- If we could snap our fingers and instantly be doing work you would love, what would you love to do?

Then ask your Guidance:

- What do you want to tell me about my passion and purpose?

The answers to these questions can give you hints about your blueprint for your passionate purpose. It's okay if nothing comes in the beginning. The more you practice Inner Bonding and develop your Loving Adult, the easier it will be to hear the answers.

Successful Dialoguing

A very important aspect of successful dialoguing is to make sure you are in a Loving Adult state. Pause and check: are you embodying a compassionate intent to learn (as a Loving Adult), or are you asking the questions from your fear and pain (your Wounded Self)? When your Wounded Self asks the questions (masking as Loving Adult), you will not be able to truly welcome and embrace your feelings, whatever they are, and the answers you receive will not be accurate. If you are not sure who is asking the questions, go back to Steps 1 and 2 before proceeding.

Listening to the Answers

After posing questions from your Loving Adult state, when you are ready to hear the answers, move your attention into your body. You want to allow the answers to come either from deep within your core self, or *through* your mind, rather than *from* your mind.

It's important to
make a commitment
to yourself, a
commitment to love.
The more we do our
inner work and move
into love for ourselves
and each other,
the more we
help our planet.

MARGARET & ERIKA

Daily
Practice

Quick Summary

LETS BRING EVERYTHING WE'VE TALKED ABOUT TOGETHER AND BRIEFLY GO THROUGH THE PROCESS.

STEP 1
Become mindful of your feelings. Decide that you want 100% responsibility for the ways in which you may be causing your own pain, and for creating your own peace and joy.

STEP 2
Choose the intent to learn to love yourself and others. Making this choice opens your heart, allows Guidance in and moves you into your Loving Adult self.

STEP 3
Compassionately dialogue with your Inner Child to discover how you are treating yourself or what you are telling yourself that is causing your wounded pain. Explore your gifts and what brings joy to your essential self.

Dialogue with your Wounded Self, exploring your false beliefs and the resulting behaviors that may be causing your pain.

STEP 4
Dialogue with your spiritual Guidance, discovering the truth and loving action for yourself.

STEP 5
Take the loving action learned in Step Four.

STEP 6
Evaluate the effectiveness of your loving action.

FOR THE FULL PROCESS, CHECK OUT THE SIX STEPS TAB

SITUATION: Overwhelmed at work   DATE 7/11

. . . .

STEP **1**

Be Willing to Take Responsibility for All of Your Feelings

Follow your breath, letting it bring **awareness to your body's sensations.**
Your Loving Adult asks your Inner Child:

WHAT ARE YOU PHYSICALLY FEELING RIGHT NOW?

*tight throat, pressure In my chest
I take 100% responsibility for these feelings!*

STEP **2**

Move into the Intent to Learn

Invite the love, strength, wisdom of Spirit into your heart and consciously choose curiosity about **what you may be doing or not doing that is causing wounded pain** while embracing any core pain. **Reminder:** Do the Anger Process if your anger is in the way of opening. See page 26.

NOTE DOWN THE INVITATION:

*I invite guidance into my heart
and choose curiousity ♡♡*

STEP **3**

Dialogue with Inner Child & Wounded Self

Put your hands on your heart. Explore your feelings, behaviors, false beliefs, and memories with love and compassion. Your Loving Adult asks your Inner Child:
How am I behaving when operating as the Wounded Self, that is causing you pain?

NOTE DOWN RESPONSES FROM YOUR INNER CHILD:

*You are pressuring me to work
harder and stay silent about
needing help. You're freaking
me out! You yell at me that
we'll get in trouble if we tell
the boss we need help.
This feels awful!*

Loving Adult asks the Wounded Self: **What are your beliefs that are causing this behavior?** What is the fear of feeling the core pain?

NOTE DOWN RESPONSES FROM THE WOUNDED SELF:

We should work harder and keep mouth shut! If the boss finds out we can't do the project, we'll get fired, just like dad did when we were little. Life will be horrible !!!

STEP 4

Dialogue with Guidance

Loving Adult asks Guidance: **What is the truth about this situation;** about the false beliefs from Step 3?

NOTE DOWN THE RESPONSE FROM GUIDANCE:

This situation is nothing like the past. Being honest with your boss is professional. If something unpredictable happens, we can deal with it!

Loving Adult asks Guidance: **What loving action(s) can I take?**

NOTE DOWN THE RESPONSE FROM GUIDANCE:

Email your boss tomorrow, ask for a meeting to discuss the project timeline and invite others to help.

STEP 5

Take Loving Action

CAN YOU TAKE THE LOVING ACTION? If no, write when you **plan to do it.**

I'll draft the email tonight, send it tomorrow at 8:00 am. Keep it short and to the point.

STEP 6

Evaluate Your Action

Even if you can't take the loving action now, you can imagine it and go back to physical sensations from Step 1. Loving Adult asks Inner Child: **What am I feeling as a result of the loving action that I took or imagined taking?**

WRITE DOWN WHAT CHANGED.

Feeling lighter in my chest and throat is open! My IC is happy! :)

SITUATION: .... DATE

....

STEP 1

Be Willing to Take Responsibility for All of Your Feelings

Follow your breath, letting it bring **awareness to your body's sensations.**
Your Loving Adult asks your Inner Child:

WHAT ARE YOU PHYSICALLY FEELING RIGHT NOW?

STEP 2

Move into the Intent to Learn

Invite the love, strength, wisdom of Spirit into your heart and consciously choose curiosity about **what you may be doing or not doing that is causing wounded pain** while embracing any core pain. **Reminder:** Do the Anger Process if your anger is in the way of opening. See page 26.

NOTE DOWN THE INVITATION:

STEP 3

Dialogue with Inner Child & Wounded Self

Put your hands on your heart. Explore your feelings, behaviors, false beliefs, and memories with love and compassion. Your Loving Adult asks your Inner Child:
How am I behaving when operating as the Wounded Self, that is causing you pain?

NOTE DOWN RESPONSES FROM YOUR INNER CHILD:

Loving Adult asks the Wounded Self: **What are your beliefs that are causing this behavior?** What is the fear of feeling the core pain?

NOTE DOWN RESPONSES FROM THE WOUNDED SELF:

STEP

4

Dialogue with Guidance

Loving Adult asks Guidance: **What is the truth about this situation**; about the false beliefs from Step 3?

NOTE DOWN THE RESPONSE FROM GUIDANCE:

Loving Adult asks Guidance: **What loving action(s) can I take?**

NOTE DOWN THE RESPONSE FROM GUIDANCE:

STEP

5

Take Loving Action

CAN YOU TAKE THE LOVING ACTION? If no, write when you **plan to do it.**

STEP

6

Evaluate Your Action

Even if you can't take the loving action now, you can imagine it and go back to physical sensations from Step 1. Loving Adult asks Inner Child: **What am I feeling as a result of the loving action that I took or imagined taking?**

WRITE DOWN WHAT CHANGED.

STEP
1

Be Willing to Take Responsibility for All of Your Feelings

Follow your breath, letting it bring **awareness to your body's sensations.**
Your Loving Adult asks your Inner Child:
WHAT ARE YOU PHYSICALLY FEELING RIGHT NOW?

STEP
2

Move into the Intent to Learn

Invite the love, strength, wisdom of Spirit into your heart and consciously choose curiosity about **what you may be doing or not doing that is causing wounded pain** while embracing any core pain. **Reminder:** Do the Anger Process if your anger is in the way of opening. See page 26.
NOTE DOWN THE INVITATION:

STEP
3

Dialogue with Inner Child & Wounded Self

Put your hands on your heart. Explore your feelings, behaviors, false beliefs, and memories with love and compassion. Your Loving Adult asks your Inner Child:
How am I behaving when operating as the Wounded Self, that is causing you pain?
NOTE DOWN RESPONSES FROM YOUR INNER CHILD:

Loving Adult asks the Wounded Self: **What are your beliefs that are causing this behavior?** What is the fear of feeling the core pain?

NOTE DOWN RESPONSES FROM THE WOUNDED SELF:

STEP
4
Dialogue with Guidance

Loving Adult asks Guidance: **What is the truth about this situation**; about the false beliefs from Step 3?

NOTE DOWN THE RESPONSE FROM GUIDANCE:

Loving Adult asks Guidance: **What loving action(s) can I take?**

NOTE DOWN THE RESPONSE FROM GUIDANCE:

STEP
5
Take Loving Action

CAN YOU TAKE THE LOVING ACTION? If no, write when you **plan to do it.**

STEP
6
Evaluate Your Action

Even if you can't take the loving action now, you can imagine it and go back to physical sensations from Step 1. Loving Adult asks Inner Child: **What am I feeling as a result of the loving action that I took or imagined taking?**

WRITE DOWN WHAT CHANGED.

....

Be Willing to Take Responsibility for All of Your Feelings

Follow your breath, letting it bring **awareness to your body's sensations.**
Your Loving Adult asks your Inner Child:

WHAT ARE YOU PHYSICALLY FEELING RIGHT NOW?

Move into the Intent to Learn

Invite the love, strength, wisdom of Spirit into your heart and consciously choose curiosity about **what you may be doing or not doing that is causing wounded pain** while embracing any core pain. **Reminder:** Do the Anger Process if your anger is in the way of opening. See page 26.

NOTE DOWN THE INVITATION:

Dialogue with Inner Child & Wounded Self

Put your hands on your heart. Explore your feelings, behaviors, false beliefs, and memories with love and compassion. Your Loving Adult asks your Inner Child:
How am I behaving when operating as the Wounded Self, that is causing you pain?

NOTE DOWN RESPONSES FROM YOUR INNER CHILD:

Loving Adult asks the Wounded Self: **What are your beliefs that are causing this behavior?** What is the fear of feeling the core pain?

NOTE DOWN RESPONSES FROM THE WOUNDED SELF:

STEP
4
Dialogue with Guidance

Loving Adult asks Guidance: **What is the truth about this situation**; about the false beliefs from Step 3?

NOTE DOWN THE RESPONSE FROM GUIDANCE:

Loving Adult asks Guidance: **What loving action(s) can I take?**

NOTE DOWN THE RESPONSE FROM GUIDANCE:

STEP
5
Take Loving Action

CAN YOU TAKE THE LOVING ACTION? If no, write when you **plan to do it.**

STEP
6
Evaluate Your Action

Even if you can't take the loving action now, you can imagine it and go back to physical sensations from Step 1. Loving Adult asks Inner Child: **What am I feeling as a result of the loving action that I took or imagined taking?**

WRITE DOWN WHAT CHANGED.

SITUATION: _____ DATE

. . . .

STEP 1

Be Willing to Take Responsibility for All of Your Feelings

Follow your breath, letting it bring **awareness to your body's sensations.**
Your Loving Adult asks your Inner Child:

WHAT ARE YOU PHYSICALLY FEELING RIGHT NOW?

STEP 2

Move into the Intent to Learn

Invite the love, strength, wisdom of Spirit into your heart and consciously choose curiosity about **what you may be doing or not doing that is causing wounded pain** while embracing any core pain. **Reminder:** Do the Anger Process if your anger is in the way of opening. See page 26.

NOTE DOWN THE INVITATION:

STEP 3

Dialogue with Inner Child & Wounded Self

Put your hands on your heart. Explore your feelings, behaviors, false beliefs, and memories with love and compassion. Your Loving Adult asks your Inner Child:
How am I behaving when operating as the Wounded Self, that is causing you pain?

NOTE DOWN RESPONSES FROM YOUR INNER CHILD:

Loving Adult asks the Wounded Self: **What are your beliefs that are causing this behavior?** What is the fear of feeling the core pain?

NOTE DOWN RESPONSES FROM THE WOUNDED SELF:

STEP
4

Dialogue with Guidance

Loving Adult asks Guidance: **What is the truth about this situation**; about the false beliefs from Step 3?

NOTE DOWN THE RESPONSE FROM GUIDANCE:

Loving Adult asks Guidance: **What loving action(s) can I take?**

NOTE DOWN THE RESPONSE FROM GUIDANCE:

STEP
5

Take Loving Action

CAN YOU TAKE THE LOVING ACTION? If no, write when you **plan to do it.**

STEP
6

Evaluate Your Action

Even if you can't take the loving action now, you can imagine it and go back to physical sensations from Step 1. Loving Adult asks Inner Child: **What am I feeling as a result of the loving action that I took or imagined taking?**

WRITE DOWN WHAT CHANGED.

....

STEP 1

Be Willing to Take Responsibility for All of Your Feelings

Follow your breath, letting it bring **awareness to your body's sensations.** Your Loving Adult asks your Inner Child:

WHAT ARE YOU PHYSICALLY FEELING RIGHT NOW?

STEP 2

Move into the Intent to Learn

Invite the love, strength, wisdom of Spirit into your heart and consciously choose curiosity about **what you may be doing or not doing that is causing wounded pain** while embracing any core pain. **Reminder:** Do the Anger Process if your anger is in the way of opening. See page 26.

NOTE DOWN THE INVITATION:

STEP 3

Dialogue with Inner Child & Wounded Self

Put your hands on your heart. Explore your feelings, behaviors, false beliefs, and memories with love and compassion. Your Loving Adult asks your Inner Child: **How am I behaving when operating as the Wounded Self, that is causing you pain?**

NOTE DOWN RESPONSES FROM YOUR INNER CHILD:

Loving Adult asks the Wounded Self: **What are your beliefs that are causing this behavior?** What is the fear of feeling the core pain?

NOTE DOWN RESPONSES FROM THE WOUNDED SELF:

Dialogue with Guidance

Loving Adult asks Guidance: **What is the truth about this situation**; about the false beliefs from Step 3?

NOTE DOWN THE RESPONSE FROM GUIDANCE:

Loving Adult asks Guidance: **What loving action(s) can I take?**

NOTE DOWN THE RESPONSE FROM GUIDANCE:

Take Loving Action

CAN YOU TAKE THE LOVING ACTION? If no, write when you **plan to do it.**

Evaluate Your Action

Even if you can't take the loving action now, you can imagine it and go back to physical sensations from Step 1. Loving Adult asks Inner Child: **What am I feeling as a result of the loving action that I took or imagined taking?**

WRITE DOWN WHAT CHANGED.

SITUATION: DATE

. . . .

STEP 1

Be Willing to Take Responsibility for All of Your Feelings

Follow your breath, letting it bring **awareness to your body's sensations.**
Your Loving Adult asks your Inner Child:

WHAT ARE YOU PHYSICALLY FEELING RIGHT NOW?

STEP 2

Move into the Intent to Learn

Invite the love, strength, wisdom of Spirit into your heart and consciously choose curiosity about **what you may be doing or not doing that is causing wounded pain** while embracing any core pain. **Reminder:** Do the Anger Process if your anger is in the way of opening. See page 26.

NOTE DOWN THE INVITATION:

STEP 3

Dialogue with Inner Child & Wounded Self

Put your hands on your heart. Explore your feelings, behaviors, false beliefs, and memories with love and compassion. Your Loving Adult asks your Inner Child:
How am I behaving when operating as the Wounded Self, that is causing you pain?

NOTE DOWN RESPONSES FROM YOUR INNER CHILD:

Loving Adult asks the Wounded Self: **What are your beliefs that are causing this behavior?** What is the fear of feeling the core pain?

NOTE DOWN RESPONSES FROM THE WOUNDED SELF:

Dialogue with Guidance

Loving Adult asks Guidance: **What is the truth about this situation;** about the false beliefs from Step 3?

NOTE DOWN THE RESPONSE FROM GUIDANCE:

Loving Adult asks Guidance: **What loving action(s) can I take?**

NOTE DOWN THE RESPONSE FROM GUIDANCE:

Take Loving Action

CAN YOU TAKE THE LOVING ACTION? If no, write when you **plan to do it.**

Evaluate Your Action

Even if you can't take the loving action now, you can imagine it and go back to physical sensations from Step 1. Loving Adult asks Inner Child: **What am I feeling as a result of the loving action that I took or imagined taking?**

WRITE DOWN WHAT CHANGED.

STEP 1

Be Willing to Take Responsibility for All of Your Feelings

Follow your breath, letting it bring **awareness to your body's sensations.**
Your Loving Adult asks your Inner Child:

WHAT ARE YOU PHYSICALLY FEELING RIGHT NOW?

STEP 2

Move into the Intent to Learn

Invite the love, strength, wisdom of Spirit into your heart and consciously choose curiosity about **what you may be doing or not doing that is causing wounded pain** while embracing any core pain. **Reminder:** Do the Anger Process if your anger is in the way of opening. See page 26.

NOTE DOWN THE INVITATION:

STEP 3

Dialogue with Inner Child & Wounded Self

Put your hands on your heart. Explore your feelings, behaviors, false beliefs, and memories with love and compassion. Your Loving Adult asks your Inner Child:
How am I behaving when operating as the Wounded Self, that is causing you pain?
NOTE DOWN RESPONSES FROM YOUR INNER CHILD:

Loving Adult asks the Wounded Self: **What are your beliefs that are causing this behavior?** What is the fear of feeling the core pain?

NOTE DOWN RESPONSES FROM THE WOUNDED SELF:

Dialogue with Guidance

Loving Adult asks Guidance: **What is the truth about this situation;** about the false beliefs from Step 3?

NOTE DOWN THE RESPONSE FROM GUIDANCE:

Loving Adult asks Guidance: **What loving action(s) can I take?**

NOTE DOWN THE RESPONSE FROM GUIDANCE:

Take Loving Action

CAN YOU TAKE THE LOVING ACTION? If no, write when you **plan to do it.**

Evaluate Your Action

Even if you can't take the loving action now, you can imagine it and go back to physical sensations from Step 1. Loving Adult asks Inner Child: **What am I feeling as a result of the loving action that I took or imagined taking?**

WRITE DOWN WHAT CHANGED.

. . . .

STEP 1

Be Willing to Take Responsibility for All of Your Feelings

Follow your breath, letting it bring **awareness to your body's sensations.**
Your Loving Adult asks your Inner Child:

WHAT ARE YOU PHYSICALLY FEELING RIGHT NOW?

STEP 2

Move into the Intent to Learn

Invite the love, strength, wisdom of Spirit into your heart and consciously choose curiosity about **what you may be doing or not doing that is causing wounded pain** while embracing any core pain. **Reminder:** Do the Anger Process if your anger is in the way of opening. See page 26.

NOTE DOWN THE INVITATION:

STEP 3

Dialogue with Inner Child & Wounded Self

Put your hands on your heart. Explore your feelings, behaviors, false beliefs, and memories with love and compassion. Your Loving Adult asks your Inner Child:
How am I behaving when operating as the Wounded Self, that is causing you pain?

NOTE DOWN RESPONSES FROM YOUR INNER CHILD:

Loving Adult asks the Wounded Self: **What are your beliefs that are causing this behavior?** What is the fear of feeling the core pain?

NOTE DOWN RESPONSES FROM THE WOUNDED SELF:

4 Dialogue with Guidance

Loving Adult asks Guidance: **What is the truth about this situation**; about the false beliefs from Step 3?

NOTE DOWN THE RESPONSE FROM GUIDANCE:

Loving Adult asks Guidance: **What loving action(s) can I take?**

NOTE DOWN THE RESPONSE FROM GUIDANCE:

5 Take Loving Action

CAN YOU TAKE THE LOVING ACTION? If no, write when you **plan to do it.**

6 Evaluate Your Action

Even if you can't take the loving action now, you can imagine it and go back to physical sensations from Step 1. Loving Adult asks Inner Child: **What am I feeling as a result of the loving action that I took or imagined taking?**

WRITE DOWN WHAT CHANGED.

SITUATION: DATE

....

STEP **1**

Be Willing to Take Responsibility for All of Your Feelings

Follow your breath, letting it bring **awareness to your body's sensations.**
Your Loving Adult asks your Inner Child:

WHAT ARE YOU PHYSICALLY FEELING RIGHT NOW?

STEP **2**

Move into the Intent to Learn

Invite the love, strength, wisdom of Spirit into your heart and consciously choose curiosity about **what you may be doing or not doing that is causing wounded pain** while embracing any core pain. **Reminder:** Do the Anger Process if your anger is in the way of opening. See page 26.

NOTE DOWN THE INVITATION:

STEP **3**

Dialogue with Inner Child & Wounded Self

Put your hands on your heart. Explore your feelings, behaviors, false beliefs, and memories with love and compassion. Your Loving Adult asks your Inner Child:
How am I behaving when operating as the Wounded Self, that is causing you pain?

NOTE DOWN RESPONSES FROM YOUR INNER CHILD:

Loving Adult asks the Wounded Self: **What are your beliefs that are causing this behavior?** What is the fear of feeling the core pain?

NOTE DOWN RESPONSES FROM THE WOUNDED SELF:

STEP

4

Dialogue with Guidance

Loving Adult asks Guidance: **What is the truth about this situation**; about the false beliefs from Step 3?

NOTE DOWN THE RESPONSE FROM GUIDANCE:

Loving Adult asks Guidance: **What loving action(s) can I take?**

NOTE DOWN THE RESPONSE FROM GUIDANCE:

STEP

5

Take Loving Action

CAN YOU TAKE THE LOVING ACTION? If no, write when you **plan to do it.**

STEP

6

Evaluate Your Action

Even if you can't take the loving action now, you can imagine it and go back to physical sensations from Step 1. Loving Adult asks Inner Child: **What am I feeling as a result of the loving action that I took or imagined taking?**

WRITE DOWN WHAT CHANGED.

SITUATION: DATE

....

STEP **1**

**Be Willing to Take Responsibility
for All of Your Feelings**

Follow your breath, letting it bring **awareness to your body's sensations.**
Your Loving Adult asks your Inner Child:

WHAT ARE YOU PHYSICALLY FEELING RIGHT NOW?

STEP **2**

Move into the Intent to Learn

Invite the love, strength, wisdom of Spirit into your heart and consciously choose
curiosity about **what you may be doing or not doing that is causing wounded pain**
while embracing any core pain. **Reminder:** Do the Anger Process if your anger is in
the way of opening. See page 26.

NOTE DOWN THE INVITATION:

STEP **3**

Dialogue with Inner Child & Wounded Self

Put your hands on your heart. Explore your feelings, behaviors, false beliefs, and
memories with love and compassion. Your Loving Adult asks your Inner Child:
How am I behaving when operating as the Wounded Self, that is causing you pain?

NOTE DOWN RESPONSES FROM YOUR INNER CHILD:

Loving Adult asks the Wounded Self: **What are your beliefs that are causing this behavior?** What is the fear of feeling the core pain?

NOTE DOWN RESPONSES FROM THE WOUNDED SELF:

Dialogue with Guidance

Loving Adult asks Guidance: **What is the truth about this situation**; about the false beliefs from Step 3?

NOTE DOWN THE RESPONSE FROM GUIDANCE:

Loving Adult asks Guidance: **What loving action(s) can I take?**

NOTE DOWN THE RESPONSE FROM GUIDANCE:

Take Loving Action

CAN YOU TAKE THE LOVING ACTION? If no, write when you **plan to do it.**

Evaluate Your Action

Even if you can't take the loving action now, you can imagine it and go back to physical sensations from Step 1. Loving Adult asks Inner Child: **What am I feeling as a result of the loving action that I took or imagined taking?**

WRITE DOWN WHAT CHANGED.

. . . .

STEP
1

Be Willing to Take Responsibility for All of Your Feelings

Follow your breath, letting it bring **awareness to your body's sensations.**
Your Loving Adult asks your Inner Child:

WHAT ARE YOU PHYSICALLY FEELING RIGHT NOW?

STEP
2

Move into the Intent to Learn

Invite the love, strength, wisdom of Spirit into your heart and consciously choose curiosity about **what you may be doing or not doing that is causing wounded pain** while embracing any core pain. **Reminder:** Do the Anger Process if your anger is in the way of opening. See page 26.

NOTE DOWN THE INVITATION:

STEP
3

Dialogue with Inner Child & Wounded Self

Put your hands on your heart. Explore your feelings, behaviors, false beliefs, and memories with love and compassion. Your Loving Adult asks your Inner Child:
How am I behaving when operating as the Wounded Self, that is causing you pain?

NOTE DOWN RESPONSES FROM YOUR INNER CHILD:

Loving Adult asks the Wounded Self: **What are your beliefs that are causing this behavior?** What is the fear of feeling the core pain?

NOTE DOWN RESPONSES FROM THE WOUNDED SELF:

STEP

4
Dialogue with Guidance

Loving Adult asks Guidance: **What is the truth about this situation**; about the false beliefs from Step 3?

NOTE DOWN THE RESPONSE FROM GUIDANCE:

Loving Adult asks Guidance: **What loving action(s) can I take?**

NOTE DOWN THE RESPONSE FROM GUIDANCE:

STEP

5
Take Loving Action

CAN YOU TAKE THE LOVING ACTION? If no, write when you **plan to do it.**

STEP

6
Evaluate Your Action

Even if you can't take the loving action now, you can imagine it and go back to physical sensations from Step 1. Loving Adult asks Inner Child: **What am I feeling as a result of the loving action that I took or imagined taking?**

WRITE DOWN WHAT CHANGED.

SITUATION: DATE
. . . .

STEP
1

Be Willing to Take Responsibility for All of Your Feelings

Follow your breath, letting it bring **awareness to your body's sensations.**
Your Loving Adult asks your Inner Child:

WHAT ARE YOU PHYSICALLY FEELING RIGHT NOW?

STEP
2

Move into the Intent to Learn

Invite the love, strength, wisdom of Spirit into your heart and consciously choose curiosity about **what you may be doing or not doing that is causing wounded pain** while embracing any core pain. **Reminder:** Do the Anger Process if your anger is in the way of opening. See page 26.

NOTE DOWN THE INVITATION:

STEP
3

Dialogue with Inner Child & Wounded Self

Put your hands on your heart. Explore your feelings, behaviors, false beliefs, and memories with love and compassion. Your Loving Adult asks your Inner Child:
How am I behaving when operating as the Wounded Self, that is causing you pain?

NOTE DOWN RESPONSES FROM YOUR INNER CHILD:

Loving Adult asks the Wounded Self: **What are your beliefs that are causing this behavior?** What is the fear of feeling the core pain?

NOTE DOWN RESPONSES FROM THE WOUNDED SELF:

STEP
4
Dialogue with Guidance

Loving Adult asks Guidance: **What is the truth about this situation**; about the false beliefs from Step 3?

NOTE DOWN THE RESPONSE FROM GUIDANCE:

Loving Adult asks Guidance: **What loving action(s) can I take?**

NOTE DOWN THE RESPONSE FROM GUIDANCE:

STEP
5
Take Loving Action

CAN YOU TAKE THE LOVING ACTION? If no, write when you **plan to do it.**

STEP
6
Evaluate Your Action

Even if you can't take the loving action now, you can imagine it and go back to physical sensations from Step 1. Loving Adult asks Inner Child: **What am I feeling as a result of the loving action that I took or imagined taking?**

WRITE DOWN WHAT CHANGED.

SITUATION: DATE

. . . .

STEP
1

Be Willing to Take Responsibility for All of Your Feelings

Follow your breath, letting it bring **awareness to your body's sensations.**
Your Loving Adult asks your Inner Child:

WHAT ARE YOU PHYSICALLY FEELING RIGHT NOW?

STEP
2

Move into the Intent to Learn

Invite the love, strength, wisdom of Spirit into your heart and consciously choose curiosity about **what you may be doing or not doing that is causing wounded pain** while embracing any core pain. **Reminder:** Do the Anger Process if your anger is in the way of opening. See page 26.

NOTE DOWN THE INVITATION:

STEP
3

Dialogue with Inner Child & Wounded Self

Put your hands on your heart. Explore your feelings, behaviors, false beliefs, and memories with love and compassion. Your Loving Adult asks your Inner Child:
How am I behaving when operating as the Wounded Self, that is causing you pain?

NOTE DOWN RESPONSES FROM YOUR INNER CHILD:

Loving Adult asks the Wounded Self: **What are your beliefs that are causing this behavior?** What is the fear of feeling the core pain?

NOTE DOWN RESPONSES FROM THE WOUNDED SELF:

STEP **4**

Dialogue with Guidance

Loving Adult asks Guidance: **What is the truth about this situation;** about the false beliefs from Step 3?

NOTE DOWN THE RESPONSE FROM GUIDANCE:

Loving Adult asks Guidance: **What loving action(s) can I take?**

NOTE DOWN THE RESPONSE FROM GUIDANCE:

STEP **5**

Take Loving Action

CAN YOU TAKE THE LOVING ACTION? If no, write when you **plan to do it.**

STEP **6**

Evaluate Your Action

Even if you can't take the loving action now, you can imagine it and go back to physical sensations from Step 1. Loving Adult asks Inner Child: **What am I feeling as a result of the loving action that I took or imagined taking?**

WRITE DOWN WHAT CHANGED.

SITUATION: DATE

....

STEP 1

Be Willing to Take Responsibility for All of Your Feelings

Follow your breath, letting it bring **awareness to your body's sensations.**
Your Loving Adult asks your Inner Child:

WHAT ARE YOU PHYSICALLY FEELING RIGHT NOW?

STEP 2

Move into the Intent to Learn

Invite the love, strength, wisdom of Spirit into your heart and consciously choose curiosity about **what you may be doing or not doing that is causing wounded pain** while embracing any core pain. **Reminder:** Do the Anger Process if your anger is in the way of opening. See page 26.

NOTE DOWN THE INVITATION:

STEP 3

Dialogue with Inner Child & Wounded Self

Put your hands on your heart. Explore your feelings, behaviors, false beliefs, and memories with love and compassion. Your Loving Adult asks your Inner Child:
How am I behaving when operating as the Wounded Self, that is causing you pain?

NOTE DOWN RESPONSES FROM YOUR INNER CHILD:

Loving Adult asks the Wounded Self: **What are your beliefs that are causing this behavior?** What is the fear of feeling the core pain?

NOTE DOWN RESPONSES FROM THE WOUNDED SELF:

STEP

4
Dialogue with Guidance

Loving Adult asks Guidance: **What is the truth about this situation**; about the false beliefs from Step 3?

NOTE DOWN THE RESPONSE FROM GUIDANCE:

Loving Adult asks Guidance: **What loving action(s) can I take?**

NOTE DOWN THE RESPONSE FROM GUIDANCE:

STEP

5
Take Loving Action

CAN YOU TAKE THE LOVING ACTION? If no, write when you **plan to do it.**

STEP

6
Evaluate Your Action

Even if you can't take the loving action now, you can imagine it and go back to physical sensations from Step 1. Loving Adult asks Inner Child: **What am I feeling as a result of the loving action that I took or imagined taking?**

WRITE DOWN WHAT CHANGED.

. . . .

STEP
1

Be Willing to Take Responsibility for All of Your Feelings

Follow your breath, letting it bring **awareness to your body's sensations.**
Your Loving Adult asks your Inner Child:
WHAT ARE YOU PHYSICALLY FEELING RIGHT NOW?

STEP
2

Move into the Intent to Learn

Invite the love, strength, wisdom of Spirit into your heart and consciously choose curiosity about **what you may be doing or not doing that is causing wounded pain** while embracing any core pain. **Reminder:** Do the Anger Process if your anger is in the way of opening. See page 26.
NOTE DOWN THE INVITATION:

STEP
3

Dialogue with Inner Child & Wounded Self

Put your hands on your heart. Explore your feelings, behaviors, false beliefs, and memories with love and compassion. Your Loving Adult asks your Inner Child:
How am I behaving when operating as the Wounded Self, that is causing you pain?
NOTE DOWN RESPONSES FROM YOUR INNER CHILD:

Loving Adult asks the Wounded Self: **What are your beliefs that are causing this behavior?** What is the fear of feeling the core pain?

NOTE DOWN RESPONSES FROM THE WOUNDED SELF:

4 Dialogue with Guidance

Loving Adult asks Guidance: **What is the truth about this situation**; about the false beliefs from Step 3?

NOTE DOWN THE RESPONSE FROM GUIDANCE:

Loving Adult asks Guidance: **What loving action(s) can I take?**

NOTE DOWN THE RESPONSE FROM GUIDANCE:

5 Take Loving Action

CAN YOU TAKE THE LOVING ACTION? If no, write when you **plan to do it.**

6 Evaluate Your Action

Even if you can't take the loving action now, you can imagine it and go back to physical sensations from Step 1. Loving Adult asks Inner Child: **What am I feeling as a result of the loving action that I took or imagined taking?**

WRITE DOWN WHAT CHANGED.

SITUATION: DATE

....

STEP
1
Be Willing to Take Responsibility for All of Your Feelings
Follow your breath, letting it bring **awareness to your body's sensations.**
Your Loving Adult asks your Inner Child:
WHAT ARE YOU PHYSICALLY FEELING RIGHT NOW?

STEP
2
Move into the Intent to Learn
Invite the love, strength, wisdom of Spirit into your heart and consciously choose curiosity about **what you may be doing or not doing that is causing wounded pain** while embracing any core pain. **Reminder:** Do the Anger Process if your anger is in the way of opening. See page 26.
NOTE DOWN THE INVITATION:

STEP
3
Dialogue with Inner Child & Wounded Self
Put your hands on your heart. Explore your feelings, behaviors, false beliefs, and memories with love and compassion. Your Loving Adult asks your Inner Child:
How am I behaving when operating as the Wounded Self, that is causing you pain?
NOTE DOWN RESPONSES FROM YOUR INNER CHILD:

Loving Adult asks the Wounded Self: **What are your beliefs that are causing this behavior?** What is the fear of feeling the core pain?

NOTE DOWN RESPONSES FROM THE WOUNDED SELF:

STEP
4

Dialogue with Guidance

Loving Adult asks Guidance: **What is the truth about this situation**; about the false beliefs from Step 3?

NOTE DOWN THE RESPONSE FROM GUIDANCE:

Loving Adult asks Guidance: **What loving action(s) can I take?**

NOTE DOWN THE RESPONSE FROM GUIDANCE:

STEP
5

Take Loving Action

CAN YOU TAKE THE LOVING ACTION? If no, write when you **plan to do it.**

STEP
6

Evaluate Your Action

Even if you can't take the loving action now, you can imagine it and go back to physical sensations from Step 1. Loving Adult asks Inner Child: **What am I feeling as a result of the loving action that I took or imagined taking?**

WRITE DOWN WHAT CHANGED.

SITUATION: DATE

. . . .

STEP **1**

Be Willing to Take Responsibility for All of Your Feelings

Follow your breath, letting it bring **awareness to your body's sensations.**
Your Loving Adult asks your Inner Child:
WHAT ARE YOU PHYSICALLY FEELING RIGHT NOW?

STEP **2**

Move into the Intent to Learn

Invite the love, strength, wisdom of Spirit into your heart and consciously choose curiosity about **what you may be doing or not doing that is causing wounded pain** while embracing any core pain. **Reminder:** Do the Anger Process if your anger is in the way of opening. See page 26.
NOTE DOWN THE INVITATION:

STEP **3**

Dialogue with Inner Child & Wounded Self

Put your hands on your heart. Explore your feelings, behaviors, false beliefs, and memories with love and compassion. Your Loving Adult asks your Inner Child:
How am I behaving when operating as the Wounded Self, that is causing you pain?
NOTE DOWN RESPONSES FROM YOUR INNER CHILD:

Loving Adult asks the Wounded Self: **What are your beliefs that are causing this behavior?** What is the fear of feeling the core pain?

NOTE DOWN RESPONSES FROM THE WOUNDED SELF:

STEP

4

Dialogue with Guidance

Loving Adult asks Guidance: **What is the truth about this situation**; about the false beliefs from Step 3?

NOTE DOWN THE RESPONSE FROM GUIDANCE:

Loving Adult asks Guidance: **What loving action(s) can I take?**

NOTE DOWN THE RESPONSE FROM GUIDANCE:

STEP

5

Take Loving Action

CAN YOU TAKE THE LOVING ACTION? If no, write when you **plan to do it.**

STEP

6

Evaluate Your Action

Even if you can't take the loving action now, you can imagine it and go back to physical sensations from Step 1. Loving Adult asks Inner Child: **What am I feeling as a result of the loving action that I took or imagined taking?**

WRITE DOWN WHAT CHANGED.

··

STEP 1

Be Willing to Take Responsibility for All of Your Feelings

Follow your breath, letting it bring **awareness to your body's sensations.**
Your Loving Adult asks your Inner Child:

WHAT ARE YOU PHYSICALLY FEELING RIGHT NOW?

STEP 2

Move into the Intent to Learn

Invite the love, strength, wisdom of Spirit into your heart and consciously choose curiosity about **what you may be doing or not doing that is causing wounded pain** while embracing any core pain. **Reminder:** Do the Anger Process if your anger is in the way of opening. See page 26.

NOTE DOWN THE INVITATION:

STEP 3

Dialogue with Inner Child & Wounded Self

Put your hands on your heart. Explore your feelings, behaviors, false beliefs, and memories with love and compassion. Your Loving Adult asks your Inner Child:
How am I behaving when operating as the Wounded Self, that is causing you pain?

NOTE DOWN RESPONSES FROM YOUR INNER CHILD:

Loving Adult asks the Wounded Self: **What are your beliefs that are causing this behavior?** What is the fear of feeling the core pain?

NOTE DOWN RESPONSES FROM THE WOUNDED SELF:

<table><tr><td>STEP
4</td><td>### Dialogue with Guidance
Loving Adult asks Guidance: **What is the truth about this situation**; about the false beliefs from Step 3?

NOTE DOWN THE RESPONSE FROM GUIDANCE:</td></tr></table>

Loving Adult asks Guidance: **What loving action(s) can I take?**

NOTE DOWN THE RESPONSE FROM GUIDANCE:

<table><tr><td>STEP
5</td><td>### Take Loving Action
CAN YOU TAKE THE LOVING ACTION? If no, write when you **plan to do it.**</td></tr></table>

<table><tr><td>STEP
6</td><td>### Evaluate Your Action
Even if you can't take the loving action now, you can imagine it and go back to physical sensations from Step 1. Loving Adult asks Inner Child: **What am I feeling as a result of the loving action that I took or imagined taking?**

WRITE DOWN WHAT CHANGED.</td></tr></table>

SITUATION: DATE

....

STEP 1

Be Willing to Take Responsibility for All of Your Feelings

Follow your breath, letting it bring **awareness to your body's sensations.**
Your Loving Adult asks your Inner Child:

WHAT ARE YOU PHYSICALLY FEELING RIGHT NOW?

STEP 2

Move into the Intent to Learn

Invite the love, strength, wisdom of Spirit into your heart and consciously choose curiosity about **what you may be doing or not doing that is causing wounded pain** while embracing any core pain. **Reminder:** Do the Anger Process if your anger is in the way of opening. See page 26.

NOTE DOWN THE INVITATION:

STEP 3

Dialogue with Inner Child & Wounded Self

Put your hands on your heart. Explore your feelings, behaviors, false beliefs, and memories with love and compassion. Your Loving Adult asks your Inner Child:
How am I behaving when operating as the Wounded Self, that is causing you pain?

NOTE DOWN RESPONSES FROM YOUR INNER CHILD:

Loving Adult asks the Wounded Self: **What are your beliefs that are causing this behavior?** What is the fear of feeling the core pain?

NOTE DOWN RESPONSES FROM THE WOUNDED SELF:

STEP
4

Dialogue with Guidance

Loving Adult asks Guidance: **What is the truth about this situation;** about the false beliefs from Step 3?

NOTE DOWN THE RESPONSE FROM GUIDANCE:

Loving Adult asks Guidance: **What loving action(s) can I take?**

NOTE DOWN THE RESPONSE FROM GUIDANCE:

STEP
5

Take Loving Action

CAN YOU TAKE THE LOVING ACTION? If no, write when you **plan to do it.**

STEP
6

Evaluate Your Action

Even if you can't take the loving action now, you can imagine it and go back to physical sensations from Step 1. Loving Adult asks Inner Child: **What am I feeling as a result of the loving action that I took or imagined taking?**

WRITE DOWN WHAT CHANGED.

SITUATION: DATE

STEP
1
Be Willing to Take Responsibility for All of Your Feelings

Follow your breath, letting it bring **awareness to your body's sensations.**
Your Loving Adult asks your Inner Child:
WHAT ARE YOU PHYSICALLY FEELING RIGHT NOW?

STEP
2
Move into the Intent to Learn

Invite the love, strength, wisdom of Spirit into your heart and consciously choose curiosity about **what you may be doing or not doing that is causing wounded pain** while embracing any core pain. **Reminder:** Do the Anger Process if your anger is in the way of opening. See page 26.
NOTE DOWN THE INVITATION:

STEP
3
Dialogue with Inner Child & Wounded Self

Put your hands on your heart. Explore your feelings, behaviors, false beliefs, and memories with love and compassion. Your Loving Adult asks your Inner Child:
How am I behaving when operating as the Wounded Self, that is causing you pain?
NOTE DOWN RESPONSES FROM YOUR INNER CHILD:

Loving Adult asks the Wounded Self: **What are your beliefs that are causing this behavior?** What is the fear of feeling the core pain?

NOTE DOWN RESPONSES FROM THE WOUNDED SELF:

STEP
Dialogue with Guidance

4

Loving Adult asks Guidance: **What is the truth about this situation**; about the false beliefs from Step 3?

NOTE DOWN THE RESPONSE FROM GUIDANCE:

Loving Adult asks Guidance: **What loving action(s) can I take?**

NOTE DOWN THE RESPONSE FROM GUIDANCE:

STEP
Take Loving Action

5

CAN YOU TAKE THE LOVING ACTION? If no, write when you **plan to do it.**

STEP
Evaluate Your Action

6

Even if you can't take the loving action now, you can imagine it and go back to physical sensations from Step 1. Loving Adult asks Inner Child: **What am I feeling as a result of the loving action that I took or imagined taking?**

WRITE DOWN WHAT CHANGED.

SITUATION:

· ·

STEP
1

Be Willing to Take Responsibility for All of Your Feelings

Follow your breath, letting it bring **awareness to your body's sensations.**
Your Loving Adult asks your Inner Child:
WHAT ARE YOU PHYSICALLY FEELING RIGHT NOW?

STEP
2

Move into the Intent to Learn

Invite the love, strength, wisdom of Spirit into your heart and consciously choose curiosity about **what you may be doing or not doing that is causing wounded pain** while embracing any core pain. **Reminder:** Do the Anger Process if your anger is in the way of opening. See page 26.
NOTE DOWN THE INVITATION:

STEP
3

Dialogue with Inner Child & Wounded Self

Put your hands on your heart. Explore your feelings, behaviors, false beliefs, and memories with love and compassion. Your Loving Adult asks your Inner Child:
How am I behaving when operating as the Wounded Self, that is causing you pain?
NOTE DOWN RESPONSES FROM YOUR INNER CHILD:

Loving Adult asks the Wounded Self: **What are your beliefs that are causing this behavior?** What is the fear of feeling the core pain?

NOTE DOWN RESPONSES FROM THE WOUNDED SELF:

STEP
4 Dialogue with Guidance

Loving Adult asks Guidance: **What is the truth about this situation;** about the false beliefs from Step 3?

NOTE DOWN THE RESPONSE FROM GUIDANCE:

Loving Adult asks Guidance: **What loving action(s) can I take?**

NOTE DOWN THE RESPONSE FROM GUIDANCE:

STEP
5 Take Loving Action

CAN YOU TAKE THE LOVING ACTION? If no, write when you **plan to do it.**

STEP
6 Evaluate Your Action

Even if you can't take the loving action now, you can imagine it and go back to physical sensations from Step 1. Loving Adult asks Inner Child: **What am I feeling as a result of the loving action that I took or imagined taking?**

WRITE DOWN WHAT CHANGED.

SITUATION: DATE

....

STEP 1

Be Willing to Take Responsibility for All of Your Feelings

Follow your breath, letting it bring **awareness to your body's sensations.**
Your Loving Adult asks your Inner Child:

WHAT ARE YOU PHYSICALLY FEELING RIGHT NOW?

STEP 2

Move into the Intent to Learn

Invite the love, strength, wisdom of Spirit into your heart and consciously choose curiosity about **what you may be doing or not doing that is causing wounded pain** while embracing any core pain. **Reminder:** Do the Anger Process if your anger is in the way of opening. See page 26.

NOTE DOWN THE INVITATION:

STEP 3

Dialogue with Inner Child & Wounded Self

Put your hands on your heart. Explore your feelings, behaviors, false beliefs, and memories with love and compassion. Your Loving Adult asks your Inner Child: **How am I behaving when operating as the Wounded Self, that is causing you pain?**

NOTE DOWN RESPONSES FROM YOUR INNER CHILD:

Loving Adult asks the Wounded Self: **What are your beliefs that are causing this behavior?** What is the fear of feeling the core pain?

NOTE DOWN RESPONSES FROM THE WOUNDED SELF:

4 Dialogue with Guidance

Loving Adult asks Guidance: **What is the truth about this situation;** about the false beliefs from Step 3?

NOTE DOWN THE RESPONSE FROM GUIDANCE:

Loving Adult asks Guidance: **What loving action(s) can I take?**

NOTE DOWN THE RESPONSE FROM GUIDANCE:

STEP

5 Take Loving Action

CAN YOU TAKE THE LOVING ACTION? If no, write when you **plan to do it.**

STEP

6 Evaluate Your Action

Even if you can't take the loving action now, you can imagine it and go back to physical sensations from Step 1. Loving Adult asks Inner Child: **What am I feeling as a result of the loving action that I took or imagined taking?**

WRITE DOWN WHAT CHANGED.

STEP
1

Be Willing to Take Responsibility for All of Your Feelings

Follow your breath, letting it bring **awareness to your body's sensations.**
Your Loving Adult asks your Inner Child:

WHAT ARE YOU PHYSICALLY FEELING RIGHT NOW?

STEP
2

Move into the Intent to Learn

Invite the love, strength, wisdom of Spirit into your heart and consciously choose curiosity about **what you may be doing or not doing that is causing wounded pain** while embracing any core pain. **Reminder:** Do the Anger Process if your anger is in the way of opening. See page 26.

NOTE DOWN THE INVITATION:

STEP
3

Dialogue with Inner Child & Wounded Self

Put your hands on your heart. Explore your feelings, behaviors, false beliefs, and memories with love and compassion. Your Loving Adult asks your Inner Child:
How am I behaving when operating as the Wounded Self, that is causing you pain?

NOTE DOWN RESPONSES FROM YOUR INNER CHILD:

Loving Adult asks the Wounded Self: **What are your beliefs that are causing this behavior?** What is the fear of feeling the core pain?

NOTE DOWN RESPONSES FROM THE WOUNDED SELF:

STEP
4
Dialogue with Guidance

Loving Adult asks Guidance: **What is the truth about this situation**; about the false beliefs from Step 3?

NOTE DOWN THE RESPONSE FROM GUIDANCE:

Loving Adult asks Guidance: **What loving action(s) can I take?**

NOTE DOWN THE RESPONSE FROM GUIDANCE:

STEP
5
Take Loving Action

CAN YOU TAKE THE LOVING ACTION? If no, write when you **plan to do it.**

STEP
6
Evaluate Your Action

Even if you can't take the loving action now, you can imagine it and go back to physical sensations from Step 1. Loving Adult asks Inner Child: **What am I feeling as a result of the loving action that I took or imagined taking?**

WRITE DOWN WHAT CHANGED.

· ·

STEP 1

Be Willing to Take Responsibility for All of Your Feelings

Follow your breath, letting it bring **awareness to your body's sensations.**
Your Loving Adult asks your Inner Child:

WHAT ARE YOU PHYSICALLY FEELING RIGHT NOW?

STEP 2

Move into the Intent to Learn

Invite the love, strength, wisdom of Spirit into your heart and consciously choose curiosity about **what you may be doing or not doing that is causing wounded pain** while embracing any core pain. **Reminder:** Do the Anger Process if your anger is in the way of opening. See page 26.

NOTE DOWN THE INVITATION:

STEP 3

Dialogue with Inner Child & Wounded Self

Put your hands on your heart. Explore your feelings, behaviors, false beliefs, and memories with love and compassion. Your Loving Adult asks your Inner Child:
How am I behaving when operating as the Wounded Self, that is causing you pain?

NOTE DOWN RESPONSES FROM YOUR INNER CHILD:

Loving Adult asks the Wounded Self: **What are your beliefs that are causing this behavior?** What is the fear of feeling the core pain?

NOTE DOWN RESPONSES FROM THE WOUNDED SELF:

4 Dialogue with Guidance

Loving Adult asks Guidance: **What is the truth about this situation**; about the false beliefs from Step 3?

NOTE DOWN THE RESPONSE FROM GUIDANCE:

Loving Adult asks Guidance: **What loving action(s) can I take?**

NOTE DOWN THE RESPONSE FROM GUIDANCE:

5 Take Loving Action

CAN YOU TAKE THE LOVING ACTION? If no, write when you **plan to do it.**

6 Evaluate Your Action

Even if you can't take the loving action now, you can imagine it and go back to physical sensations from Step 1. Loving Adult asks Inner Child: **What am I feeling as a result of the loving action that I took or imagined taking?**

WRITE DOWN WHAT CHANGED.

. . . .

STEP
1

Be Willing to Take Responsibility for All of Your Feelings

Follow your breath, letting it bring **awareness to your body's sensations.**
Your Loving Adult asks your Inner Child:

WHAT ARE YOU PHYSICALLY FEELING RIGHT NOW?

STEP
2

Move into the Intent to Learn

Invite the love, strength, wisdom of Spirit into your heart and consciously choose curiosity about **what you may be doing or not doing that is causing wounded pain** while embracing any core pain. **Reminder:** Do the Anger Process if your anger is in the way of opening. See page 26.

NOTE DOWN THE INVITATION:

STEP
3

Dialogue with Inner Child & Wounded Self

Put your hands on your heart. Explore your feelings, behaviors, false beliefs, and memories with love and compassion. Your Loving Adult asks your Inner Child:
How am I behaving when operating as the Wounded Self, that is causing you pain?

NOTE DOWN RESPONSES FROM YOUR INNER CHILD:

Loving Adult asks the Wounded Self: **What are your beliefs that are causing this behavior?** What is the fear of feeling the core pain?

NOTE DOWN RESPONSES FROM THE WOUNDED SELF:

STEP **4**

Dialogue with Guidance

Loving Adult asks Guidance: **What is the truth about this situation;** about the false beliefs from Step 3?

NOTE DOWN THE RESPONSE FROM GUIDANCE:

Loving Adult asks Guidance: **What loving action(s) can I take?**

NOTE DOWN THE RESPONSE FROM GUIDANCE:

STEP **5**

Take Loving Action

CAN YOU TAKE THE LOVING ACTION? If no, write when you **plan to do it.**

STEP **6**

Evaluate Your Action

Even if you can't take the loving action now, you can imagine it and go back to physical sensations from Step 1. Loving Adult asks Inner Child: **What am I feeling as a result of the loving action that I took or imagined taking?**

WRITE DOWN WHAT CHANGED.

STEP 1

Be Willing to Take Responsibility for All of Your Feelings

Follow your breath, letting it bring **awareness to your body's sensations.**
Your Loving Adult asks your Inner Child:

WHAT ARE YOU PHYSICALLY FEELING RIGHT NOW?

STEP 2

Move into the Intent to Learn

Invite the love, strength, wisdom of Spirit into your heart and consciously choose curiosity about **what you may be doing or not doing that is causing wounded pain** while embracing any core pain. **Reminder:** Do the Anger Process if your anger is in the way of opening. See page 26.

NOTE DOWN THE INVITATION:

STEP 3

Dialogue with Inner Child & Wounded Self

Put your hands on your heart. Explore your feelings, behaviors, false beliefs, and memories with love and compassion. Your Loving Adult asks your Inner Child:
How am I behaving when operating as the Wounded Self, that is causing you pain?
NOTE DOWN RESPONSES FROM YOUR INNER CHILD:

Loving Adult asks the Wounded Self: **What are your beliefs that are causing this behavior?** What is the fear of feeling the core pain?

NOTE DOWN RESPONSES FROM THE WOUNDED SELF:

STEP
4 ## Dialogue with Guidance

Loving Adult asks Guidance: **What is the truth about this situation**; about the false beliefs from Step 3?

NOTE DOWN THE RESPONSE FROM GUIDANCE:

Loving Adult asks Guidance: **What loving action(s) can I take?**

NOTE DOWN THE RESPONSE FROM GUIDANCE:

STEP
5 ## Take Loving Action

CAN YOU TAKE THE LOVING ACTION? If no, write when you **plan to do it.**

STEP
6 ## Evaluate Your Action

Even if you can't take the loving action now, you can imagine it and go back to physical sensations from Step 1. Loving Adult asks Inner Child: **What am I feeling as a result of the loving action that I took or imagined taking?**

WRITE DOWN WHAT CHANGED.

....

STEP
1

Be Willing to Take Responsibility for All of Your Feelings

Follow your breath, letting it bring **awareness to your body's sensations.**
Your Loving Adult asks your Inner Child:

WHAT ARE YOU PHYSICALLY FEELING RIGHT NOW?

STEP
2

Move into the Intent to Learn

Invite the love, strength, wisdom of Spirit into your heart and consciously choose curiosity about **what you may be doing or not doing that is causing wounded pain** while embracing any core pain. **Reminder:** Do the Anger Process if your anger is in the way of opening. See page 26.

NOTE DOWN THE INVITATION:

STEP
3

Dialogue with Inner Child & Wounded Self

Put your hands on your heart. Explore your feelings, behaviors, false beliefs, and memories with love and compassion. Your Loving Adult asks your Inner Child:
How am I behaving when operating as the Wounded Self, that is causing you pain?

NOTE DOWN RESPONSES FROM YOUR INNER CHILD:

Loving Adult asks the Wounded Self: **What are your beliefs that are causing this behavior?** What is the fear of feeling the core pain?

NOTE DOWN RESPONSES FROM THE WOUNDED SELF:

STEP
4 ## Dialogue with Guidance

Loving Adult asks Guidance: **What is the truth about this situation**; about the false beliefs from Step 3?

NOTE DOWN THE RESPONSE FROM GUIDANCE:

Loving Adult asks Guidance: **What loving action(s) can I take?**

NOTE DOWN THE RESPONSE FROM GUIDANCE:

STEP
5 ## Take Loving Action

CAN YOU TAKE THE LOVING ACTION? If no, write when you **plan to do it.**

STEP
6 ## Evaluate Your Action

Even if you can't take the loving action now, you can imagine it and go back to physical sensations from Step 1. Loving Adult asks Inner Child: **What am I feeling as a result of the loving action that I took or imagined taking?**

WRITE DOWN WHAT CHANGED.

. . . .

STEP **1**

Be Willing to Take Responsibility for All of Your Feelings

Follow your breath, letting it bring **awareness to your body's sensations.**
Your Loving Adult asks your Inner Child:

WHAT ARE YOU PHYSICALLY FEELING RIGHT NOW?

STEP **2**

Move into the Intent to Learn

Invite the love, strength, wisdom of Spirit into your heart and consciously choose curiosity about **what you may be doing or not doing that is causing wounded pain** while embracing any core pain. **Reminder:** Do the Anger Process if your anger is in the way of opening. See page 26.

NOTE DOWN THE INVITATION:

STEP **3**

Dialogue with Inner Child & Wounded Self

Put your hands on your heart. Explore your feelings, behaviors, false beliefs, and memories with love and compassion. Your Loving Adult asks your Inner Child:
How am I behaving when operating as the Wounded Self, that is causing you pain?

NOTE DOWN RESPONSES FROM YOUR INNER CHILD:

Loving Adult asks the Wounded Self: **What are your beliefs that are causing this behavior?** What is the fear of feeling the core pain?

NOTE DOWN RESPONSES FROM THE WOUNDED SELF:

STEP 4

Dialogue with Guidance

Loving Adult asks Guidance: **What is the truth about this situation;** about the false beliefs from Step 3?

NOTE DOWN THE RESPONSE FROM GUIDANCE:

Loving Adult asks Guidance: **What loving action(s) can I take?**

NOTE DOWN THE RESPONSE FROM GUIDANCE:

STEP 5

Take Loving Action

CAN YOU TAKE THE LOVING ACTION? If no, write when you **plan to do it.**

STEP 6

Evaluate Your Action

Even if you can't take the loving action now, you can imagine it and go back to physical sensations from Step 1. Loving Adult asks Inner Child: **What am I feeling as a result of the loving action that I took or imagined taking?**

WRITE DOWN WHAT CHANGED.

. . . .

STEP
1

Be Willing to Take Responsibility for All of Your Feelings

Follow your breath, letting it bring **awareness to your body's sensations.**
Your Loving Adult asks your Inner Child:

WHAT ARE YOU PHYSICALLY FEELING RIGHT NOW?

STEP
2

Move into the Intent to Learn

Invite the love, strength, wisdom of Spirit into your heart and consciously choose
curiosity about **what you may be doing or not doing that is causing wounded pain**
while embracing any core pain. **Reminder:** Do the Anger Process if your anger is in
the way of opening. See page 26.

NOTE DOWN THE INVITATION:

STEP
3

Dialogue with Inner Child & Wounded Self

Put your hands on your heart. Explore your feelings, behaviors, false beliefs, and
memories with love and compassion. Your Loving Adult asks your Inner Child:
How am I behaving when operating as the Wounded Self, that is causing you pain?

NOTE DOWN RESPONSES FROM YOUR INNER CHILD:

Loving Adult asks the Wounded Self: **What are your beliefs that are causing this behavior?** What is the fear of feeling the core pain?

NOTE DOWN RESPONSES FROM THE WOUNDED SELF:

STEP 4

Dialogue with Guidance

Loving Adult asks Guidance: **What is the truth about this situation**; about the false beliefs from Step 3?

NOTE DOWN THE RESPONSE FROM GUIDANCE:

Loving Adult asks Guidance: **What loving action(s) can I take?**

NOTE DOWN THE RESPONSE FROM GUIDANCE:

STEP 5

Take Loving Action

CAN YOU TAKE THE LOVING ACTION? If no, write when you **plan to do it.**

STEP 6

Evaluate Your Action

Even if you can't take the loving action now, you can imagine it and go back to physical sensations from Step 1. Loving Adult asks Inner Child: **What am I feeling as a result of the loving action that I took or imagined taking?**

WRITE DOWN WHAT CHANGED.

SITUATION: DATE

··

1

Be Willing to Take Responsibility for All of Your Feelings

Follow your breath, letting it bring **awareness to your body's sensations.**
Your Loving Adult asks your Inner Child:

WHAT ARE YOU PHYSICALLY FEELING RIGHT NOW?

STEP
2

Move into the Intent to Learn

Invite the love, strength, wisdom of Spirit into your heart and consciously choose curiosity about **what you may be doing or not doing that is causing wounded pain** while embracing any core pain. **Reminder:** Do the Anger Process if your anger is in the way of opening. See page 26.

NOTE DOWN THE INVITATION:

STEP
3

Dialogue with Inner Child & Wounded Self

Put your hands on your heart. Explore your feelings, behaviors, false beliefs, and memories with love and compassion. Your Loving Adult asks your Inner Child:
How am I behaving when operating as the Wounded Self, that is causing you pain?
NOTE DOWN RESPONSES FROM YOUR INNER CHILD:

Loving Adult asks the Wounded Self: **What are your beliefs that are causing this behavior?** What is the fear of feeling the core pain?

NOTE DOWN RESPONSES FROM THE WOUNDED SELF:

STEP

4

Dialogue with Guidance

Loving Adult asks Guidance: **What is the truth about this situation;** about the false beliefs from Step 3?

NOTE DOWN THE RESPONSE FROM GUIDANCE:

Loving Adult asks Guidance: **What loving action(s) can I take?**

NOTE DOWN THE RESPONSE FROM GUIDANCE:

STEP

5

Take Loving Action

CAN YOU TAKE THE LOVING ACTION? If no, write when you **plan to do it.**

STEP

6

Evaluate Your Action

Even if you can't take the loving action now, you can imagine it and go back to physical sensations from Step 1. Loving Adult asks Inner Child: **What am I feeling as a result of the loving action that I took or imagined taking?**

WRITE DOWN WHAT CHANGED.

SITUATION: DATE

....

STEP 1

Be Willing to Take Responsibility for All of Your Feelings

Follow your breath, letting it bring **awareness to your body's sensations.**
Your Loving Adult asks your Inner Child:

WHAT ARE YOU PHYSICALLY FEELING RIGHT NOW?

STEP 2

Move into the Intent to Learn

Invite the love, strength, wisdom of Spirit into your heart and consciously choose curiosity about **what you may be doing or not doing that is causing wounded pain** while embracing any core pain. **Reminder:** Do the Anger Process if your anger is in the way of opening. See page 26.

NOTE DOWN THE INVITATION:

STEP 3

Dialogue with Inner Child & Wounded Self

Put your hands on your heart. Explore your feelings, behaviors, false beliefs, and memories with love and compassion. Your Loving Adult asks your Inner Child:
How am I behaving when operating as the Wounded Self, that is causing you pain?

NOTE DOWN RESPONSES FROM YOUR INNER CHILD:

Loving Adult asks the Wounded Self: **What are your beliefs that are causing this behavior?** What is the fear of feeling the core pain?

NOTE DOWN RESPONSES FROM THE WOUNDED SELF:

STEP 4 — Dialogue with Guidance

Loving Adult asks Guidance: **What is the truth about this situation;** about the false beliefs from Step 3?

NOTE DOWN THE RESPONSE FROM GUIDANCE:

Loving Adult asks Guidance: **What loving action(s) can I take?**

NOTE DOWN THE RESPONSE FROM GUIDANCE:

STEP 5 — Take Loving Action

CAN YOU TAKE THE LOVING ACTION? If no, write when you **plan to do it.**

STEP 6 — Evaluate Your Action

Even if you can't take the loving action now, you can imagine it and go back to physical sensations from Step 1. Loving Adult asks Inner Child: **What am I feeling as a result of the loving action that I took or imagined taking?**

WRITE DOWN WHAT CHANGED.

Letting your
Inner Child know
that you are loved
is one of the greatest
gifts you can give
to yourself.
Take the loving
actions!

MARGARET & ERIKA

Notes

Introduction
to Notes

....

THE NOTES INVITE YOU TO KEEP
RUNNING LISTS OF YOUR PRACTICE.

CAPTURE THE RADIANT AND UNIQUE
QUALITIES OF YOUR ESSENCE.

JOT DOWN THE MOMENTS WHEN
YOU FEEL MOST CONNECTED TO
YOUR INNER TRUTH AND DESCRIBE
HOW YOU ENVISION YOUR GUIDANCE.

CHRONICLE THE NUDGES OF
GUIDANCE THAT STEER YOU TOWARDS
TAKING LOVING ACTIONS.

KEEP AN INVENTORY OF THE
FALSE BELIEFS SO YOU CAN GO BACK AND
DEEPEN THE HEALING PROCESS.

MAKE NOTE OF THE
COURAGEOUS STEPS YOU TAKE.

AND, MOST IMPORTANTLY,
ENJOY YOURSELF!

Characteristics of My Inner Child:

WHAT DOES GUIDANCE SAY ARE THE INNATE TRAITS OF MY INNER CHILD?

I Feel Most Connected to My Inner Child When:

Description of My Guidance:

WHAT DOES MY GUIDANCE LOOK / SOUND / FEEL LIKE?

I Feel Most Connected to My Guidance When . . .

False Beliefs I Uncovered in My Inner Bonding Practice:

KEEP A LIST OF FALSE BELIEFS YOU'VE UNCOVERED

Loving Actions I Am Planning to Take:

KEEP A LIST OF LOVING ACTIONS
YOU'VE LEARNED FROM GUIDANCE

Situations I
Want to Work On:

Other Notes:

Be conscious of
choosing who you
want to be—loving
or unloving, open or
closed, in surrender to
Spirit or attempting
to control, protecting
against pain or
learning about love.

MARGARET & ERIKA

About the
Authors
+
Resources

Creative Synergy

. . . .

THIS JOURNAL IS A COLLABORATION
BETWEEN CO-CREATORS OF INNER BONDING,
DR MARGARET PAUL AND DR ERIKA CHOPICH,
AND COURAGEOUS BEING,
A CONSCIOUS LEADERSHIP CENTER.

OUR WISH IS FOR THESE PAGES
TO SERVE YOU AS A SACRED SPACE WHERE
YOU CAN PRACTICE SELF-FACILITATING,
AND DOCUMENT THE PROFOUND DISCOVERIES
YOU MAKE AS YOU DIVE INTO THE
DEPTHS OF THE TRANSFORMATIVE
SIX-STEPS PROCESS.

TO DOWNLOAD BLANK TEMPLATES OF THE
PRACTICE SPREADS, SCAN THIS QR CODE

Dr. Margaret Paul

Dr. Paul is the author/co-author of several best-selling books, including *Do I Have To Give Up Me to Be Loved By You?*, *Inner Bonding*, *Healing Your Aloneness*, *The Healing Your Aloneness Workbook*, *Do I Have To Give Up Me to Be Loved By My Kids?*, and *Do I Have To Give Up Me To Be Loved By God?* Dr. Paul's books have been distributed around the world and have been translated into eleven languages.

Margaret holds a PhD in Psychology and is a relationship expert, noted public speaker, workshop leader, educator, Chaplain, consultant and artist. She has appeared on many radio and TV shows, including the Oprah Winfrey Show. She has successfully worked with thousands of individuals, couples, and businesses and has been teaching classes and seminars since 1967.

Margaret continues to work with individuals and couples throughout the world—mostly virtually. She is able to access spiritual Guidance during her sessions, which enables her to work with people wherever they are in the world. Her current passion is working on and developing content for the Inner Bonding website, as well as distributing SelfQuest®, the software program that teaches Inner Bonding®. It is donated to prisons and schools, as well as sold to the general public.

Margaret is passionate about evolving and teaching the process of Inner Bonding, and helping people rapidly heal the root causes of their pain and discover their path to joy and loving relationships.

In her spare time, Margaret loves to paint, make pottery, take photos, watch birds, read, ride horses, and spend time with her grandchildren.

Dr. Erika Chopich

Dr. Chopich holds a PhD in Psychology, is a best-selling author, and an ordained Chaplain. She has worked extensively with homeless populations around the country. Erika has a medical background, and before practicing as a psychotherapist, she served as an administrator for the Los Angeles Free Clinic.

In addition to working with individuals, groups, and business mediation, Erika is an accomplished speaker and seminar leader. She has appeared on many radio and TV shows, including the Oprah Winfrey Show. She is co-author of *Healing Your Aloneness* and the *Healing Your Aloneness Workbook*, which have been translated into seven languages and are bestsellers in Germany.

Erika currently resides in Berthoud, Colorado. She is an accomplished pilot and an experienced chef. She continually offers her insight, creativity, quick wit, humor and playfulness to the ever-evolving process of Inner Bonding. In addition, her unique ability to see and speak with spiritual Guidance supports the Inner Bonding process with a constant source of new information.

Erika is passionate about helping people heal with horses. She has tremendous experience with equine-assisted therapy, ranch experience, nutritional facilitation, and utilizes Inner Bonding in her successful work with children, adolescents, and adults suffering from trauma, abuse, and grief, including children with autism.

Courageous Being

Ivana Polonijo, PhD

Ivana has been encouraging other humans to value and express their Inner Child since first grade, when she helped another little girl stand up to bullies. She blends a Ph.D. in Anthropology, executive experience from 15+ years in finance and non-profit boards service, with inner-work facilitation training. She founded Courageous Being, a conscious leadership center focused on empowering women+ and allies to humanize the world of business and speed up the much-needed DEIB progress. The center's transformative processes are steeped in Inner Bonding, which we believe is the key conscious leadership technique that can bring about positive shifts in the business setting. Learn more at **www.courageousbeing.com**.

Kristin Anderson

Kristin is a freelance graphic designer with a specialty in branding and packaging. She is a collaborator, strategist, and sounding board who brings form and color to ideas and dreams . . . and a cheerleader for those who are bringing positive change into the world.

Liam Polonijo

Liam is an avid Inner Bonding practitioner. Through committed daily practice, he has upleveled his leadership, communication, organization, time-management skills, and navigation of personal and professional transitions. Liam serves as Generation Z Consultant to Courageous Being, providing valuable input across the center's varied services. He is a psychology major at the University of Colorado Boulder.

Resources

. . . .

Inner Bonding Website: innerbonding.com

Dr. Margaret Paul's Inner Bonding Podcast: Available on most popular podcast platforms and at: innerbonding.com/show-page/129/inner-bonding-podcasts.html

Inner Bonding Masterclass: Twice a month in this live Masterclass, Dr. Margaret brings you through an Inner Bonding process, speaking on a topic, and then doing laser sessions with some participants. innerbondinghub.com/sp/membership/

Free Inner Bonding Course: innerbonding.com/welcome

Inner Bonding Foundation Course: Learn to Facilitate Yourself through the Six Steps: innerbonding.com/show-page/371/inner-bonding-foundation-course.html

Thirty-Day Inner Bonding e-Courses: "Love Yourself," "Attracting Your Beloved," "Wildly, Deeply, Joyously in Love!," "Frequency," "Passionate Purpose, Vibrant Health," and more: innerbonding.com/show-page/159/home-study-courses.html

SelfQuest: The Inner Bonding in-depth online program: selfquest.com

Inner Bonding Facilitator Training Program: Become a certified Inner Bonding facilitator: innerbonding.com/show-page/91/facilitator-training.html

Books, lectures, workshops, webinars, e-books and more: innerbonding.com/store.php

Events, workshops, intensives, and support groups: innerbonding.com/events.php

Sign up for free newsletter Inner Bonding Journal: innerbonding.com/show-page/352/journal-sign-up.html

9 781722 507206